SOMEBODY...Train me for MARRIAGE

A guide to marriage, for the over analytical minds

Sometimes I wonder if marriage is truly for everyone. Sometimes I ponder if it hadn't been for the fantastic tax breaks and the legitimacy of your child's existence, would most people get married? Sometimes I am amazed that people spend multiple decades together and are still going strong. But I never wonder at how beautiful this partnership and teamwork really can be. If only we can retain the beauty and purity of the first feelings that comes to us when we know that we have met the right person. Unfortunately, the institution of marriage also lies within societal parameters and influence. And external influences often are the impeding factor to this lovely union...

Contents

Why this book?

Have you ever realized that we walk through life and are continuously getting trained and groomed? Constant conditioning as we call it. We even get trained to get groomed. Society calls this being civilized.

Let's start off from the beginning. From the day you're born, you get trained at home on how to eat, sleep, sit, stand, speak, laugh, cry (or not to), make friends and how to stay away from those who are not worth being your friends... and the list goes on. Then comes school, where you are trained to be a "civilized human being" for the next thirteen years. You somehow manage to get to college and your university trains you on how expensive life can really be to call yourself educated. You then somehow get a job to finally put this ordeal of many years to good fruitful and monetary use to sustain yourself in society and get trained on-job, off-job, at home and at social gatherings.

Then you have a baby and the world inundates you with books, life lessons and support groups on how to be the best parent. I think I received five identical gifts for my baby shower "What to expect when you are expecting". Sometimes I wish one of them said "What not to expect when you become a parent". Then comes the time when you even go to the extent of going to Barnes and Nobles to buy the next edition- "What to expect when they are toddlers". I personally didn't go through these books myself, hence my knowledge of sequels is limited, but one of you must know if there is something to the tune of "What to expect when they turn pre-teens" or "What to expect when they are in their horrible teens". Well, I spared myself all of those and I am not ashamed to say it.

Then life happens and you realize that your marriage was just not worth it and not something you want to invest any more of your superbly positive energy in. You then do the unthinkable. You venture out to the attorney's office and get stormed by all the steps involved in getting yourself out of a relationship which has taken a toll on your life. And while you are wheeling under the process of financial, psychological, emotional and physical separation, you also get presented with a mandatory training required to get the final paper that says you are an individual who can breathe free (again). You now have to go through training…or probably two. If you have that beautiful child for whom you got trained to be the best parent, you now have to go through the training which broadly speaking says – 'Training for families in transition'. And then, of course, you have to go through the 'Training for Adults for Divorce'. The latter trains you how to think as an individual again. It also teaches you to treat yourself and your ex-spouse as humans who can again co-exist on planet Earth.

Life has a way of making you cynical without you realizing you have shed all your good manners. After all the training received in life, the ones received during the divorce proceedings were probably the most useful in relationship management.

As I was getting trained to be divorced, I realized somewhere society had missed on an essential step of TRAINING ME FOR MY MARRIAGE! For all the trainings received in life, nobody told me where to go to make sure I had earned my marriage certificate. They made me go through thirteen years of school + five years of undergraduate school + two years of graduate school to earn the food that I eat and the house where I stay. Twenty years of excruciating pain to make sure that I can afford something better than the $1 meal which sometimes I have to cook myself. But nobody had the courtesy of giving me a short six hours tutorial on what to do when I have to share that meal or home with the person I marry.

If I now say this to my mother, she will be very quick to remind me that the training time is the dating period. That's when you get to know the person, find synergies between your likes and dislikes and think you can grow old and senile with that one person. And that's how I was supposed to find out if I am ready to wake up next to one person for the rest of my life or not.

If I could spend $50 to get trained on how to start treating a person I have lived with for twelve years as a human again (part of the divorce procedure - you have to get trained on 'Transition for Families'), I would have gladly spent more than that to train me on how to do that right for the first twelve years itself. It just might have saved me the $50 later. (Caution: divorces are much more expensive than that but that's insurance, and the training is skillset acquisition.

So, having now exposed to you my scratched, bruised and brutally tortured heart, I ask again...where the hell is that training for couples to know what they are signing up for when they saunter into the Marriage Bureau to get your marriage certificate? (That was just so easy, it was pretty scary. I walked in and fifteen minutes later, I had a piece of paper that said that in one months' time, I will sign my whole individuality away).

You are getting married…

So, you found the right person. You feel it deep in your heart that this is the right person. You feel it deep in your guts that this is the right person. You also think you have now found the right person. Hence, your mind, heart and gut/instinct tells you that you hit the jackpot. You feel happy, ecstatic, special and gorgeous from inside and out. You feel like you are walking two inches above ground level. You know that your mom will be proud of your choice. You know that you dad will be proud that you are settling down. But all in all, you did well. You also feel sneakily good because you are now the envy of your friends and the topic of all the good natured ridicule from closer friends. This is your day. This is your time.

You start planning your wedding. Correction: statistically speaking, 82.3% of married couples should say "We started planning for our wedding that we are holding for everybody else but us". Yes, that cynical side again.

Engaged couples, you need to start thinking selfishly. The day is meant to be YOURS. Not your parents, your grandparents, your neighbors, your friends, your colleagues (unless it's a strategic social alliance you are getting yourself into). And this day is definitely not your associates whom you invite to fill up chairs or the room to save face. The day signifies the legal endorsement and societal stamp of approval that you can now share health insurance, bequeath your property as you truly want or ascertain your child doesn't get called a "bastard" when they are smart enough to understand the true meaning of the word. And on a nicer side, this day signifies your promise to another person of love, lust, luxurious monogamous sex and commitment to growing old together.

But with a probabilistic approach of 82.3%, you are not committing that day to the person you love but to everybody else and everybody around including the wallpaper! Why would you want to do that to yourself and to another human being? Why go to the extent of calling your spouse "*The* significant other"?

A young colleague of mine opened my eye for me to this reality. She was getting married to her longtime boyfriend/man friend, who was finally divorced and was ready to commit again. Don't know if it was his wisdom or her desire not to spend too much money or her smartness in life, but she decided on a small, cozy marriage just for the two of them. She rented a villa in Key West, Florida. She invited their family over there. She invited her cousin who was also a reverend, who could get then married in the backyard of the villa. The family then spent a week, vacationing on the beach and city. The two families got to know each other being in close quarters for a week. After that, the newly married couple whisked away to their honeymoon, the families went their respective ways and the marriage was done. Very select friends who were invited too, probably stayed back in Key West to enjoy the true offerings of the place after the marital rigmarole was over. Brilliant!

I heard her plan, saw her implementation and was so impressed. She avoided expense, stress and unwanted chaos. She and, I am sure, he was happy taking those vows in the restroom of our office building. They were co-habituating already. Now they will have access to the privileges that the legal system allows them as a married couple and also carry the risk of either sharing some or a majority of their hard earned assets if things don't go well for their marriage. But if you block out my smart-arse comments, her plan was brilliant. She focused on her and him. She let adults be adults around them. She was not going to be drawn into emotional or psychological drama, more often than not, associated with weddings and families/friends. She took the vow to be with the man who mattered. But this plan and this execution doesn't need to be the case only when you are on a shoe string budget. You can do the same even if you have useless money coming out of your ears or if you have always dreamed of having the fairy tale wedding. The only advice here is stay FOCUSSED on the people who truly matter. The first people who matter are you and your fiancé. Then it's about the people who matter to you. The rest of the world (apologies to all of them) DO NOT.

The path to this strategy is not easy. But when is any smart strategy easy? Your family members, your friends, your loved ones, your "don't remember his name" relatives, all have something to say, do or insinuate. Block them out. They had their day. This is yours. Stick to your plan.

But you can only stick to a plan when you have one. Most people (safe to say 82.3% of married couples) do not have a plan or a clue as to what they truly want. What is truly important to you? Growing up, what did you think your D-Day will look like? By D here I mean "destiny" not "doom".

Step 1: Make a list of your dreams for the day and prioritize for your wedding.

Step 2: Live by your list, nothing less. If you get more, good for you. Do not compromise or sacrifice.

Step 3: Be Happy and enjoy the day. It's your day. Be selfish and be focused on being happy. And be focused on managing your expectations. This last part if probably the hardest, especially when it comes to expectations you might have from your fiancé. It's as much your fiancé's day as it is yours.

As silly as it sometimes sounds, writing out your ideas is not such a bad idea. You might discover that you had thoughts that you didn't realize, verbalize or accept (yet). Let your guards down. What does the eight year old in you think when he/she thinks of marriage? What does the thirteen year old in you think when he/she reached puberty went for a wedding and liked it? What does the eighteen year old in you think when she dreams of that first kiss on the wedding day?

If that list is blank, head to the nearest court house and use the judge. Even Las Vegas is not a bad idea. It's perfect if that DAY is not what's important. The PERSON standing next to you on that day is.

Getting back, make that bloody beautiful list for yourself. What do YOU want? Ask your fiancé to make that same list. You will get resistance from your fiancé if you are the bride. "That's bull shit, baby. That's for girls. You do what you want to do." Listen but don't hear. State it for the record that you will be thrilled if you get his list to be incorporated into the day meant for both of you. You also state for the record that if there is no list, no after the fact complaints or discussions will be fair or entertained. Do it now or keep your mouth shut on this subject forever. Reading facts are always so much more sustaining on the memory bank than just hearing it once. Write out your list and share with him if required to show and lead the case. But write.

While making your list, be blunt and be true to yourself. If you want electric blue shoes under your white gown, write it and then do it. If you want to make your bridesmaids wear the sleaziest, sexiest dress, do it. You will just have to find happy friends who would want to share that adventure with you.

That list can include items like venue, outfit, number of guests, quality of guests, music, noise, hair style, seating arrangement and the list goes on. But at any point, if you feel stressed (symptoms are very obvious and most marriage consenting adults should recognize that by now), STOP. Then you are not making your list, you are making somebody else's list. Your list that has things about your dreams and your wishes cannot make you stressed. Stop and think. Are you transitioning from things you want to things everybody has either told you that you want or that everybody else wants? Hope it's not your conditioning that is taking over that list now. Let it be YOUR list. Your truth and your life.

Selfishness in this case is just the best ingredient. You are about to enter a "lifelong" commitment. Know what you want out of this deal and make yourself happy. Focus on yourself first. If you and your significant other's list cause stress, stop and think about the aspects that cause conflict. Do they matter to you? Would giving that up, cause you to think you missed something when you are ten years down the lane, twenty years down the lane? If not, then that item was truly not a fit in that list. If it will cause you unhappiness down the lane, tell your fiancé. If you strike that item off your list, you will not be doing that because you love your fiancé. You will be registering in your brain that you just made a sacrifice and a compromise. Those two lethal words are the start of your journey towards unhappiness.

But in making the list, please don't put items for the sake of putting them. If so, STOP again. Are you taking this marriage seriously? Please take marriage seriously. It is the worst formulated contract devised by human society at large but one that might very well have consequences on innocent lives including those you don't even know will exist in the future.

Once the list is done, once the two of you have found your mutually inclusive list, let that be the jargon. Hopefully neither of you feel like your heartfelt items were struck out. Hopefully you now know what that D-Day will look like, smell like and feel like.

If you do have money to spare, think about hiring a wedding planner, hand the list over to the person/company and vanish. Appear as guests for the wedding, smile and enjoy. Why I say hire versus ask/ request somebody you know, is because money makes people committed. Your wedding planner better live up to your wish list. Your mom's friend or your favorite aunt just might inject "a few favorite things" of yours that they think you might like. Nope. You have stated in black and white what you want, your plan is ready, somebody needs to go and implement it. Your part is now to go and enjoy the day as if that was the U2 concert in Dublin that you went from Tulsan, OK to attend and will never forget for the rest of your life (that's the day you fell in love with the person you are about to marry). Some ask me how you can "just" attend your own marriage. Yes you can and yes you should. That day is a celebration of you and your love coming together in marital harmony. That's all you need to be worried about. Not the food, the glamor, the invitees and the arrangements. You just need to be worried about the celebration of your love.

If you don't have money to spare but have a list of things that they want, get a reality check. Either you wait, save and then get that D-Day or try to think about what is more important. Marrying the person you want to or marry the person you want to and then keep thinking about the amount of debt you took on to have that ONE day. Alternatively, look at that list and see if you can still achieve all of that by using some inexpensive options. Examples would be: if you want a Bahamas vacation. Ask yourself. Do you want a Bahamas vacation or do you want a beautiful beach with white sand. Do you want to give the Gulf Shores a shot? If it was me, and I wanted a Bahamas vacation wedding, but cannot afford, I would stop and postpone the wedding and start saving like crazy. Here is why. I would get to the Gulf Shores and get married. But seven years into the marriage, when all of a sudden a flat screen TV appears on my door step because my husband wanted that, but my new green satin dress wasn't ordered, the conversation somehow will drag to a lost dream of a Bahamas vacation wedding without me fully realizing it. I would register the dream of the Bahamas vacation wedding as something I gave to my husband as a gift for which there is no full appreciation or attempt to repay. Call me crass, call me selfish but if something was this important to me and I didn't address it, shame on me for not trying. And instead of blaming myself, I will end up blaming the "better half of my life" for either not making it up to me or for not making me realize that it was very important to my psyche.

So, in essence, we have now covered the following:

1. You have no list, which suggests; you just love your fiancé and want to be with him/her *today*. Another special day is not going to be so important or will not change anything in your life and the way you feel about him.

2. You have a list and have enough money to make it happen on limited resources. Go for it. That is essentially your priority list and you are ready to leap into happiness with the things you want and that truly matter.

3. You have a list and the money to take care of things. Hire a wedding planner, hand over the list and come back on wedding day. Ease your mind. Enjoy that day. You paid for it.

4. You have a list but the length of which doesn't match the breath of your wallet. Save and revisit D-Day. If that convergence of dreams and means cannot happen in the practical foreseeable future, look for relatively inexpensive alternatives. Actually, ask yourself for a true priority list and see if you can live with in ten to twenty years later.

Now, relax and enjoy your wedding day. You have earned it. But remember, even if you want to etch it on the back of your hand, that day is for you and for your fiancé. Nobody else matters. If there are people who have emotional or egotistical conniptions, please smile and ask them to take it away from you and your surroundings. Be selfish and be mean if necessary. But be happy. That day is for you and will be etched in your memory forever. Make it a happy memory. You owe it to yourself.

Ending this lovely beginning story, will cite another wedding of another colleague of mine. This beautiful young lady wanted to have the quintessential movie style themed wedding. With

Kentucky Derby themed everything from decorations to toilet paper rolls, it was really a dream wedding, but for me and the rest of the 200 guests who attended. She gained weight due to the stress during the planning process, her bank balance was drawn down by ~$30k (her spend to income was a teeth grinding ratio) and she still had things that could make it a little bit better and a little bit more exotic but she had to "compromise" on her dreams. I remember spending three hours looking for the best Derby themed gift from her registered list. Three years later, she was back in Kentucky from Michigan (where she had moved to after wedding). She was now divorced with a bunch load of Derby themed items that she couldn't fit into her newly rented apartment and had bitter memories of all the things that went wrong on her wedding day instead of everything that was perfect. I am sure those bitter memories had been expressed several times before they were fully shared with us in the office. So much for the significance of D Day.

Your Honeymoon...

Punchline here is don't miss your honeymoon for anything. Take as much time as you can afford. You will treasure this memory. But more importantly, you will need these memories to fall back to when you have bad days in your marriage. And please don't let anybody try to convince you that marriage is only a bed of roses. You will have bad days.

If you take a minute to think about why the concept originated society at large and especially those who have been experienced in the beautiful institution called marriage, knew that it can be difficult and trying. The start is when the two participants in this agreement are most vulnerable but also most in love with each other to go ahead with this big step. With the iron smoldering hot for the true amalgamation of the union to take place, what better time to get out and cocoon yourself in a faraway place where no family would bother you and no friend would be around to add flavors to your personal days? Two souls get away and create memories which nobody can take away from them ever.

The very concept of exploring each other in a legitimate legal way with societal stamp of approval also makes it different and somewhat appealing in a sensual scintillating manner. Thus far, if you were dating, your societal environment would have given you a thumbs-up as of approval but you knew there was a lingering question. Will this lead somewhere fruitful, aka a legitimate relationship with legal parameters involved? Actually in layman's language, the society was secretly wondering if that dating relationship was going to lead to a place where they get to have their power play and give their stamp of approval. It's all about power and all about control at the end of the day when it comes to human society and civilization as we know it today. If you went away on vacations during the dating timeframe, upon return, you probably faced the unspoken questions from your "well-wishers" about if this trip meant it was becoming a little bit more serious and heading a little bit towards to "I-Dos". And yes, you didn't realize it but you felt that mental pressure from everybody about the fact that life's ultimate success comes when you tie the knot with the love of your life.

But the beauty of a honeymoon is that you went on the same vacation (probably) but now society at large is wishing you their best and hoping that you bring back naughty stories and beautiful pictures (and some small gifts) from exotic locations. They have done their duty and exercised their God given right to endorse your union with a legal sanctity. So, now you can legitimately have unadulterated fun and not feel the mental pressure you otherwise would have. But so what? A system was created, you abided by it but now you are with the person who truly matters.

Honeymoons are the best time to really feel free and feel connected. Enjoy the view, enjoy yourself and enjoy your spouse. Again, be selfish and do what the two of you really want to do. Get drunk, be sober, and enjoy sex that you always did, explore the venue but more than anything else explore yourself. This is the time the world shuts down and you exist in a world that has two people. You and your spouse. The rest of the world needs to dilute for the two of you during this time.

A few items to remember. Let go of your phone, your Facebook account, your LinkedIn page, your snap chat account et al. Those will still exist when you get back to reality.

Then let go of trying to reach back to family to update them about your whereabouts. As long as you are safe and healthy, nobody should care or want to care about what you are doing, except for the person with you on that honeymoon.

The sky is blue and the grass is green. You are now synched with the soul and psyche of the person with you.

Why is that important? Because many years from now when you feel like your marriage is reaching a plateau and you don't know what to do about it, you will either look back at this vacation or recall all the fun memories that you two created. Or you will pick up your bags and head out for a similar vacation (hopefully with the same person) to recreate those memories.

The honeymoon is when you are learning to block the rest of the world out. Married couples struggle with this one aspect as you learn if you read on. You need to learn to block the rest of the world out sometimes at least to find each other and truly be with each other.

Here are a few things that might come your way to block you from this honeymoon:

1. *The time is not right as there are other family commitments. But we will take the honeymoon a month from the day of the wedding.* STOP. You just said that the family is a priority and your new marriage is not. IS that truly how you want to start a new life with the love of your

life? Get your bags packed and go. Family commitments don't stop for the rest of your life, but your one month gap is always going to be part of your history. Your energy level will be different one month later. You would have already had your one month of being a married couple in the society. Your wedding excitement would have dissipated one month later. It's like saying I will start constructing the foundation of the building but stop midway to put a window standing nearby and then come back to finish the foundation. Who the hell wants to see the window standing? I want my foundation truly done so that I can start building my structure on it.

2. *We are busy right now and need to get back to work. The wedding planning and the wedding itself already caused me to take time off work. I really can't afford to take more right now. But in six months' time, I will have the courage to ask my boss for additional time to head out for my honeymoon.* STOP. You might as well say I don't want to go for my honeymoon at all. The time you take off six months later to head out will not be a honeymoon but will be another vacation. You will take plenty of those through the course of your life. You only get that one shot at your

honeymoon after (this) marriage...take it. If you think time is going to be a constraint, manage it. Cut short the wedding planning time frame, work overtime such that you can take the time off after the wedding. Do not compromise on this time. It will haunt you forever. And heaven forbid if you don't get time off for this honeymoon right now but your new spouse does. Do you think your spouse won't remind you of the lack of commitment to the start of your marriage later on when the right argument comes up? Oh, dear friend, you better be prepared. Those fights when they happen and God knows they will, you would have just dealt away a few more cards than you needed to lose at that game. For working professionals, the analogy can be that you start your new job and on the first day of work, your new boss wants to take you out for lunch. But instead you would like to stay back and clean up your office since you really want to do that on your first day and there is no other time than the lunch hour to do that. Don't refuse that first day lunch with the boss. Your office can wait.

3. *We don't have enough money now to head out for the honeymoon destination that we both want to go to. We will save some more and then take that dream honeymoon.*

STOP. Plan better. If you think you won't have the money for the honeymoon since you spent that entire mullah on your wedding day, then you didn't plan the wedding properly. Cut down your guest list, trim down on the décor, don't invite those whom you haven't seen in the past two years and don't intend to for the next few. Consider your options. Don't do anything that will make you move away from your wedding wish list but take away the fluff and the fat to save up for that honeymoon. Another option is to start planning ahead and looking for deals. Use online travel sites that allow you to book ahead of time at discounted rates. Also look out for destinations similar to the one that the two of you had discussed but a little bit more economical. Instead of the Bora Bora honeymoon, can you settle for the Riviera? You have to be true to yourself and to your new spouse or then fiancé about it. But at least explore that option. Maybe you can go to the Riviera right now and head to Bora Bora for honeymoon version 2 when you have saved more.

So now you have addressed the three main constraints that arise throughout the rest of your life. Time, money and circumstances (I would love to say society but I am sure somewhere I am inviting a backlash from conformists). With the right intent and the right open conversation with your partner in crime in this instance. Be open and be truthful about keeping the sanctity of cocooning yourselves in your new world.

You have also realized that it is not about just going out for the honeymoon. A honeymoon taken two weeks after your wedding day is not a honeymoon. It is then a vacation. A honeymoon is taken right after your wedding.

You are running away, eloping with your love to 'Neverland' where nobody can reach you. And here is how I define nobody: The noise that comes into your lives (with all the good or bad intentions). Noise does permeate into your life. It will be in the form of friends and families wanting to sit down and talk about the wedding and how it went. They would want to discuss the styles, the textures, the demeanors, the attitudes, the food, the décor etc. of your D-Day. You don't need to hear all that yet. You had your day. It was yours and nobody has the right to put the positive or negative energy into your brains through their words, actions or expressions (nonverbal is even more lethal at times than the verbal ones).

Noise is also in the form of now having to think about your new abode together (if you were already not doing so before the wedding or if you don't intend to continue your previous arrangement). You enter the new abode and start thinking about furniture, about pictures you want to hang of the wedding, of the kitchen and how you would like to entertain as a couple now and of thank you notes that you still have to get down to. Run away from your wedding venue if you can. Go away and live in your Blue Lagoon before you start living in the new domesticated world.

When you get back from your honeymoon, all that noise will still be there, don't get me wrong. But you will carry on your face a sneaky smirk smile and in your eyes, a naughty glint, the meaning of which only one other person in this world will know the true meaning off. When your mother in law harps on the gifts given by her friend from the church and how it didn't match up to the level she expected, you will know how to tune it out. You will mentally hibernate into your Blue Lagoon and think about all the things that you have not and CANNNOT share with the rest of your family and friends. They are too naughty to be spoken off but still make the hair at the back of your neck curl up when you think about them. Actually you might even be thinking about re-enacting some of those later tonight and don't give a hoot to what your new mom-in-law's good friend gave you for your wedding. Now you have a weapon to deal with the positive or negative energy (verbal or nonverbal) that you are about to encounter for the rest of your life.

Better still, you share a fleeting glance with your spouse and you both know, that crystal vase will probably not last long in the room if you guys had your way and were re-enacting your honeymoon acts.

You are now equipped to take on the domesticated world since you now know what it is to be in your cocoon. A cocoon you share with your spouse and nobody else. Nobody.

You are domesticated now…Accept it

(But you don't really have to)

You dated, you loved, and you married. Take a pause. Smell the air and see your new world for what it is. You are now domesticated. You are about to start a fresh new life.

You have seen your mom and dad have a life as a couple but you didn't see them as individuals when they were single and free. They were not always trying to keep the home clean and tidy or making sure your next meal have all the colors available for nutrition. They too threw away their greens from the plates, ate junk food and threw their shoes across the room upon entering their apartment. You saw them as a happy couple with an immaculate home, wonderfully prepared meals and family traditions upheld. You were comfortable there. And now is your turn to make a home.

You also want to re-create the same thing. It's called proliferation of thought, induction of ideas and recreation of your mental image. You think married family home, you think about your home from your childhood. This will manifest itself in the décor you use, the food you prepare, the night time rituals you hold sacrosanct, the beer that you prefer when you are going to head for when you unwind on your couch after a whole day's work.

New Home Décor

You grew up in a picture perfect home and you recreate the same in your new home.

Now, I could be wrong. You could have grown up in a shabby place, where you mom really didn't cook or clean. But you would go to your friend's home to play and see her mom have the picture perfect household. Somewhere then you told yourself when you get married; you will not do what your mom does but make a home like Mrs. Thomas. Or you will get married to the person who will create the home for you.

Conditioning does that to you. Your brain was getting conditioned to think that way. But who are you now? Do you know? How about that little cheat sheet list again?

Are you truly your mom or your dad? Are you truly the person who wants to make sure that your panty has all the labels pointing straight and forward or the person who has the table platters and napkin rings always ready for decorative purposes? Are you truly the person who will keep firewood ready at all times or keep the yard raked and trimmed no matter what the weather? If you are, then you have it easy. You have a play book and you can play your game. You will find peace and happiness in the beauty you will create around you that will remind you of your upbringing. You are ready to let posterity cherish the continuity of sequence and progression.

But what if you are not? What if you an individual who has roamed the world and stayed in different cultures and seen a lot more of the world than your parents? And while you were globe-trotting, you picked up a different sequence of conditioning where your brain suggested that you like things that are different from how you grew up. Now instead of liking the flower patterns on our curtains, you like sleek oriental drapes with back lighting that will create sensual lighting with the flick of the remote? This is just a small example to show that don't ignore that side of you just because that's not what you grew up with. Make yourself happy. Unless you are happy, you cannot make anybody else happy.

Now consider that you are not living in the house by yourself. There is another person there with you. If you have lived with this person for some time before the marriage, you might have found your sweet spot of convergence of ideas, thoughts and other things that are more important. But once you moved into a new abode, that sweet spot might have to be revisited.

Situations to be considered: you thought you knew what your partner wanted. But being married brings untold and unspoken expectations and considerations into the equation now. It makes it all the more fun when you didn't know what your partner wanted. You had seen your partner in the rental apartment but that's all it was, a rental apartment.

Now you are ready to make home and the unspoken and untold considerations and expectations are again setting in. What does your spouse like? You are now making a home for the two of you. Everything you read or hear tells you; make a home for the two of you. That's perfect for those who really don't have much idea or vision of what they want their living environment to be like (yes, there are those of us who don't care. We have bigger better things to worry about). And then there are those who know that what they think of design is far inferior to those of your spouse and want to go with the better ideas.

Identify yourself. And try to identify your spouse's idea of a daily living environment. And have that open, honest conversation. But I can just make this one step easier for your discovery phase. It's a bloody difficult thing to do. But not impossible. Those who are truly in touch with themselves and their inner peace/happiness will be able to verbalize it eloquently.

But most of us reach that stage much later in life (not when we are starting off young and wet behind our ears). Fix it...If you know that you won't be able to do yourself or your spouse justice, there is always an easier (aka monetarily inclined) solution. Get yourself an interior designer or architect, who will listen to both of you. They are like the therapist for homes. They will objectively listen to your likes, dislikes and bring a solution for consideration that covers all or most bases. If they bring forward compromises for the two of you to consider, you always have the option to turn them down. But at the end of the day, if you move ahead with their created living space, you will feel a sense of completion. Why? Because you paid for it with your hard earned money.

Money has a way of bringing a sense of balance and maturity in your perspectives. (Remember the time you were told you have to bear your own auto insurance? Your level of commitment to your job went up exponentially. You knew that if you wanted to be out for the next Friday night out, you needed to have that car and that stupid insurance that your parents just refused to foot the bill for.) Paying for that architect/designer is your commitment to the auto insurance. Now when the home is left to the two of you, you will smile because you have said yes to the design, your individual thoughts were listened to and you paid for it ($$$$$ Kaching!!!)

If you can't afford the money for the architect/designer, consider doing the design for yourself. Two things to remember. Cut out your list of priorities. You want the blue and grey bedroom, the kitchen with bring flowery wallpaper, a small area to call your workshop, a bar area that is stacked with your favorite drinks at all times, a room converted to gym etc. Ask for a similar list from your spouse. Be open that there might be conflicting wants in those two lists. You might want the blue bedroom while your spouse wants soft pastel green. Try to either blend the two. Don't take one over the other. That's the biggest mistake. Take them all (hopefully in an aesthetically pleasing manner). If need be, get one wall blue and the other green.

But in all this merging of minds, keep your individuality. Unless you are happy, remember that you can't make the other person happy. If you think you will compromise now, you will end up using those items as ammunition in your fights later. Don't compromise on your wants and wishes. Bring them forward so that the other person knows.

Another big mistake individuals make (practically throughout life) is to think that your loved one will know what you want. You think you don't need to verbalize your wants and wishes. WRONG. They were not born to decipher your mind. They were born to decipher their own. And so were you. So DO your job.

Let your loved one know what you want.

Wrapping up this topic, let me share my experience. Being an architect, I knew what kind of living space I wanted. But I was also keenly aware that my individuality should not cloud what the family living quarters should look like. While walking down aisles of furniture stores, I realized early on that my husband liked traditional furniture and décor. Guess what I liked. All modern aesthetics.

After buying our first home, I decorated it all in traditional style. Of course, he didn't know what my style was, even though to his credit, he did ask. I concealed my likes with the thought that it will make him happy. I wanted to make him happy. Hence, our first home was all done up in southern comfort, traditional styled look and feel.

Years later, during one of the many arguments we had, I would keep telling him about the compromises I made even in my views of style and décor. How I had to live in a traditional environment when all I wanted was a modern, clean cut and clean lines styled home. He was stunned.

He had not realized and I had not told him, how much I hated that furniture. I lived with them trying to make him happy. But he much preferred that I feel comfortable and at home as he does. I compromised but I later threw it back at his face. How good was that? Several thousands of dollars and much heartache later, we were left with a house full of things that neither of us wanted. I didn't want them from the get go. He didn't want them because he would much rather avoid the stigma attached to them or the compromise being thrown back at him than live with those monstrosities.

Everybody will tell you, you can't have it all. Actually you can. If the two of you have very divergent likes and dislikes in décor (amongst other things) and you weren't able to identify that before saying "I Do", divide and conquer (in a good way). Look at your list and find rooms that are yours and those that are for your spouse. You have the kitchen while he has the bar. You get the living room while he gets the finished basement. I really don't have a good solution for the bedroom. But find room for your individuality. You get an office while she gets the parlor. You get the garage while she gets the front garden. Suppressing your wishes, thinking compromises will bring peace, only builds up a frustration inside that will find a vent sometime in the future. Only the vent might not be very controlled. It usually manifests itself in ugly words, anger and venomous verbal exchanges that leave scars and wounds for life.

Also, somewhere in that big or small house, find a room that is just for you. Where you can go and shut yourself out from the rest of the world or at least the rest of your married life. You will need it. And make it known. That room is for you alone. That's your domain, your kingdom. You don't want to share it and you will not. If you want to keep it filthy, dirty and cluttered, that's perfectly fine. If you want to paint it electric pink or violent grey, that's fine. If your spouse can't deal with that room, they need to stay out of it. But no comments or no assessments will be accepted or tolerated. In a nice way, of course. That is where you sustain your individuality. Trust me you need it.

You are cooking

Guess what, your mom and mother in law did not cook the same food in their respective kitchens. Maybe they did, but they cooked it in a different manner and had different results. Your spouse has a memory bank full of mom cooked meals as do you. Now either one of you takes over control over the kitchen or you share. You won't pick the same spices, the same ingredients or the same level of baking and you are going to learn to live with the different styles. I like slightly sour food and the rest of my family can't stand anything sour in their food. I let go of my likes to make food that they liked.

Similar to our home décor memory bank, our pallets also have likes and dislikes from our childhood. You might not know them but you feel them (especially when it doesn't feel right).

The best case scenario is your mom was a pathetic cook and you knew it. You love good food and your spouse is the best cook you know. You just hit jackpot. But like all odds, the likes of that happening is somewhat low. But if that happens, you are lucky and you should know it and appreciate it. Tell your spouse about how much you value it. Maybe that's why you chose each other to spend the rest of your lives with.

But if you didn't hit the jackpot, life doesn't stop. You love eating and you love good food. But your mom was the best cook you know. You spouse just isn't. At this point, can I ask, can you cook? Have you embodied some of the traits from your mom? If so, you think you can use them? Try owning the kitchen, if your spouse is Ok with it.

I am not a food person. I never liked cooking. But I learned. Learned because I was told that the woman of the house owns the kitchen. I didn't need to own anything. My then husband loved to eat and loved to cook. Before we got married, he cooked for himself and was perfectly happy. I came along and I brought with myself all the pre-trained thoughts that I should be the one to cook. Cook for my family. The woman who cooks, rules. Utter nonsense for sure!

I did take over the kitchen. I learned how to cook. I turned out to be a good cook. He loved my cooking. But cooking for me was a chore. It wasn't a stress relief and I didn't really enjoy being in the kitchen. I did it because I was supposed to be the queen of that domain.

Don't get me wrong. I did love decorating the kitchen but hated using it. During the initial days, we would cook together. That was kind of fun. But as my domain expertise increased, I would take the lead and soon he was sitting in the living room, watching TV while chatting with me while I cooked. Perfect scenario. But only if I loved it.

Only I didn't love it. I hated cooking but I had learned to live with it. I cooked when I didn't want. I was miserable and I usually got frustrated. My frustration manifested itself in other ways. Anger, irritation and retail therapy.

If you are in any ways like me. Be careful. Don't let societal norms sway you like it did me. Be clear that the kitchen is not your domain and not where you want expertise. If both of you don't like cooking, that's fine. Use food that is easy to put together. Save up to head out as often as you can afford. If you don't like eating out, consider letting your partner cook for you. You can make it up to him in many other (interesting) ways.

What if you don't like cooking and your partner does. If he is ok with holding the fort for the grub, let him. You can help on the periphery. Chop, clean or pour the wine for him. Watch him cook. You might find millions of ways to make yourself of use in the kitchen versus actually cooking. In fact, some of those activities (if you let your mind be a little bit more fertile, he might admire those more than wanting your nonexistent culinary skills).

If you are a food person and love to cook, experiment with recipes. Explore. Try different cuisines. Make it an adventure versus making it a chore. Why? Because it can be one of those non-verbal activities that create some special memories.

There will be times when you and your partner want different things to eat. Don't let anything stop you from doing exactly that. There are buzzing advises in your ears about how couples should eat same food, share a meal. Sharing a meal doesn't mean you have to eat something you don't want to. If you want Chinese and your partner fancies Indian, go for it. You don't have to eat Indian and your spouse doesn't need to eat Chinese. Order in. Or hit a food court that has both.

I am not asking you to compromise or settle. The more you settle when it creates internal friction for you, the more miserable you will be. And if you think you can handle your misery, it is the first step towards a downslide roller coaster that more times than not ends in the court.

The more miserable you are, the more you make everybody around you miserable. That's at home and at work. It's not about the food. It's about you not being able to do something you truly want to do.

That last statement probably sums up everything you probably keep in mind stepping into marriage. Don't do what doesn't come from within and what doesn't sit well with you inside. It's not about the food, it's not about the Indian versus Chinese, it's not about who is cooking. It's about you standing by your truth. It's about staying true to you and bringing that inner peace and smile. Once you achieve that, only then will you manage to make others around happy. Find ways and find solutions to make yourself happy. Also allow your spouse to find happiness. You need the inner smiles versus the fake hypocritical plaster smiles on your faces when you compromise.

The word compromise spills out too easily from all of us. We have been trained to think that once you compromise, you are a better bigger person. But the truthful training has not been imbibed that we weren't born to be better bigger person. We were born to be human. To seek, find and sustain happiness. Once we do that, our world opens up to making our surrounding such that we feel happiness around us.

The minute you compromise for the happiness of a loved one, you are making the other person obligated to you, at least in your mind. Making a compromise is good only when you tell yourself that you are doing this for yourself versus the other person.

Daily family traditions

You are starting a family and a new life. Traditions are one place where couples have a field day creating conflict. It starts off with couples trying to accept and adopt each other's family traditions to show assimilation. It works for many. For others, it backfires slowly, when you have other problems to deal with in marriage. How you ask? The root cause is that you have grown up with one set of traditions and your spouse with another. In many cases, you will bring two different solutions to a situation when it comes to creating a tradition for your new family. And more often than not, you will think that the solution you provide is the best one. That is when you have your conflict situations arise.

You have a conflict, you have an argument. Then to express your resentment and your displeasure, you will start avoiding somethings that are traditions that were brought in from your spouse's family. It might start as just trying to prove a point initially, but the mark will be made and once the scar sticks, you will use that as ammunition every time you get into a conflict situation. Nothing wrong, nothing abnormal. Very normal human behavior.

As I start on this topic, you have to recognize that not all off this applies for everybody. But in general, expectations of most couples from their marriages are very much on similar lines. The reason, societal conditioning that we grow up with, read books or watch movies about.

Family traditions are something you and your spouse are creating for yourselves. Some of those that you inherited from your respective families. Others, you are creating for your new family.

The traditions that you want to carry on from your respective families. Talk it out with your spouse. See if that is something your partner is OK with. If not, learn to let go. It's actually not that bloody important. Why? You might think it's very important right now but in all practicality, you want something to hand down to your kids. And trust me when I say, your kids would much rather have you guys smile than keep a tradition that may or may not stick for sustainability.

But let's accept something. You will learn to accept some traditions from family-in-law. When you do, do with a smile but also make your partner know that when the child in you wants to throw a tantrum and want to stick to childhood traditions, it should not be taken to heart. It just means the child is scared of change. And that's Okay for the child to show its reluctance.

Hopefully, you and your spouse already know that neither of you will stick to those traditions forever.

When the time for children arrives, you both will want to impart traditions from your respective family sides. That is fantastic for the child. The more the better. I would say stop for a second and see if that is correct. It's not a competition on whose side of the family, the child takes more from. And taking on traditions from one side of the family versus the other definitely doesn't translate into whose family the child will be closer to and love more. How about giving the child the opportunity to choose?

I know it sounds against common wisdom imparted to us all our lives. How many times have we heard or felt- "I wish my child had more time with my side of the family. Maybe he/she would have been closer to our family traditions and our family members." I had grown up thinking that the child will get close to whatever he or she is most exposed to. But we underestimate the child and the human bond that the child shares with family members. Let the child be. He or she will discover by themselves what it means to have family traditions and family intimacy. It is not a competition when it concerns your child. Let them be.

For those without children, yet, it is absolutely impossible to imagine what child rearing can be like. If you thought your life was difficult, your work was impossible, your career an insurmountable task, child rearing makes all of them look like the first grade math class. It is the best thing that happens to you, if you are up for it. But it is the most difficult thing you will ever do. Once a child enters the equation, life is never the same again.

So, now added to that difficulty, if you start introducing other constraints like whose family traditions should the child be absorbing more, you are just making your life more difficult. Be smart, be savvy. Focus on what is important. You are, your spouse is and your child will always be. If you start taking on small battles just to sustain something that somebody somewhere told you makes your child closer to your parents, you are bound to lose the war. And the collateral damage will be in the form of unhappiness for your immediate family or tension between you and your spouse. And good parents will recognize that as soon as the above said takes place, it gets reflected in the child's behavior. Let me give you an example of my experience. I grew up with tons of things that I had heard makes me a better person- my family traditions. I had rebelled and retaliated during my formative and nonconforming days. But once married, suddenly those traditions seemed the way to be to make sure that my child has his roots deeply anchored in culture and tradition. And the more I introduced my family traditions, the more came from my husband. Why? Because being another type A in the family, he couldn't bear the thought that our child, the one that we both had contribution in creating, would get closer to one side of the family versus the other. Result: constant turmoil. Bickering like you haven't heard before. Those traditions from the two sides weren't always mutually conducive. They too conflicted at times. How his family did things versus how my family did things weren't always the same. And my child suffered. He could feel the tension in the air, the stress all this created. He, being a child, also knew how to be a perfect diplomat. How to try to please both parents somehow by being a great actor. But what unnecessary work for a little child. After twelve years of this tug of war (amongst many other such tugs of wars), sitting with a divorce decree in hand, sometimes I wonder were they worth it? Were those traditions so sacrosanct that I gave up on a more important thing in life? My life itself.

YOUR friends and your individuality: Keep them!

They are so worth the investment. When you were single, you had your friends, your significant other had their friends and then there were mutual friends whom both of you knew. You got married. And you thought, all of that should come together. Think again. Your friends don't change. But your outlook towards them changes and that gets reflected in some of the things you in turn get back from them. Keep the lines separated. Keep them as they were.

Your friends are probably never going to be best buddies with your spouse. And you shouldn't expect them to be. They signed up for you, not the other person. But your feelings and your thoughts sometimes get reflected from your friend (especially those whom you care for). You will read the countenance of your friends and make your deductions from them. Remember the days when you would go out to date. How important was it that you get liked by your date's friends. Why do you think any of those changes once you have tied that beautiful knot of togetherness? Right or wrong, it will happen. It's natural. The best you can do is keeping those lines just as they were when you were dating.

If your significant other didn't know your school friends that well, KEEP IT THAT WAYS. Let it be casual without the expectations that your spouse will now be best buds with your 'bestie'. But sustain the friendship. Carve out time that you can spend with your friends. It is not only helpful but also therapeutic. It keeps you grounded to your own individuality and yourself. You are yourself with your friends. That aspect is extremely important when you come into a relationship where there is another person who is equally important. You need to keep yourself attuned to your true self. It's your "me time" with "me and those who made me without judging". I am of the firm belief that good friends are more valuable than all the wealth of the world. They took you for who you are and don't expect anything from you. It's for you to find those true good friends though. But for the purposes of this training, take some time out to spend with these good friends. They will rejuvenate you for your marital bliss. They will be the energy drink to your eight hour shift. They will be the listening ear when you want to speak nonsense about everything around you without being judged. They will be the quiet wisdom when you are not seeking any. They will be the reflection of your true feelings that you are too afraid to see for yourself.

Then there were mutual friends. They had probably seen you when you were dating or those whom you hung out with when you did double dates. They are also very important. They remind you of the fun you had when you were enjoying the courtship period. They are a point of reference for you for the reasons you decided on saying "I Do" to this particular person standing next to you today. They will know you in the relationship you are in. They will be a reflection of your love for each other. They will reflect some of the feelings you have now that you are married. They are important in keeping your sanity during the days when you sit back and think "what the hell was I thinking in saying yes to his proposal". These friends will also at times bring the two of you together when you are slowly drifting apart from each other, for one   reason   or   another. All this is very important in sustaining the happiness bubble that you thought you enter when you walk down that aisle. People around you help make that happen. And none better than those who are "friends". Be careful with your selection though. But that's not a training you need for marriage. That's a training you need for life in general. Your friends can sink you or help you swim. Good friends will help you rise above all to truly help you fly.

Many a times, once married, we feel this insane pull for togetherness. That is great. That is love. That is the reason you got into the nuptial situation in the first place. "Till death do us apart". But there is a long way between now and death. And you need to find some breathers once in a while. So too much togetherness can be claustrophobic and unhealthy.

Taking periodic time away from the togetherness helps us in being happy with the life-long togetherness. And that's where friends truly help. I am inclined to say, they make a better choice than many or most relatives. Even if you are close to your relatives. Friends are friends. When you go away with them, they are not sitting back and analyzing how your spouse is doing in life and your economic, social and psychological quotient. They will probably take you out for drinks and get you to a point where you all are back to the days when life was easy and anything was possible! Those were good days. No hassle free living.

Also, both of you don't have to take time off at the same time. That's not entirely necessary unless that is convenient in terms of planning and execution. Take time off when you feel like it. Plan out something independently with your friends. You have always wanted to go hiking/ mountain biking but your spouse hates the thought of walking on dangerous terrains and wilderness. In fact your spouse probably hates the thought of being out in natural environments where there is not a man-made aspect within sixty feet. Don't wait around for him/her to change their views about hiking. Take a spin on your own. Head out. Fulfill your desires and wishes. You only live once and you live it full. You really don't want to be the fifty year old with severe knee problems now, thinking about the missed opportunities of mountain hiking and biking in Yosemite. You want to sit back one evening near the fireplace, snuggled in with your loved one, sharing the experience and the joy you felt when you reached the highest point that you wanted to conquer.

There is joy in being alone as much as there is joy in being together. Finding the time to sit with a book or the music you liked when you were a teenager has value. It has value to your marriage. That's where the spatial division of real estate in the new home is important. That 'me' time in the 'me' space is important in rejuvenating your spirits and giving the other person theirs. Remember what I said before. Too much togetherness can be claustrophobic.

If you feel like being quiet and alone even with company, that's ok. If you feel like going for a drive by yourself to clear up your head, that's Ok. It doesn't mean you are rejecting your spouse. It means you are rejuvenating yourself so that you have positive energy to contribute to the marriage. If your spouse wants to go shopping alone, doesn't mean that he/she does not value your choice of clothes or fashion. It means he/she wants to explore some retail therapy.

At some point in our lives, we get conditioned into thinking of ourselves as anything but animals. We are animals. We have some similar instincts and we should tune into them time and again. Animals wander off. And then they come back. It's not that they leave their grounding habitat. It is a natural instinct to walk, explore, evolve and come back to the roots. This thought permeates in life, in the day and in the hour. Give yourself and your spouse the courtesy and the space to wander off sometimes and explore how much they have evolved.

I remember my initial days of marriage when shopping was an experience. I loved the idea of my husband finding me clothes and telling me what he thought once I tried them on. Later on in life, he complained that I didn't do as much of that with him. He wasn't wrong. He was absolutely right in feeling the way he did. The problem was that I went from one extreme to another. I would go shopping exclusively with him in the earlier days and none with him in the later. I only wish everything was in moderation. I wish I did some shopping with him, some with friends and some by myself all throughout. That would have avoided him feeling I was changing as a person. It would have avoided him feeling I didn't want him participating in somethings that were important to me. Also, my wardrobe evolved as I matured. He participated in that evolution in the initial stages but not as much as the days went by. Result- men being men had not noticed the new sheath dresses I had started experimenting with but did notice the bright red tight sheath I wore one day for my company event. The comment passed alone was inconsequential. "Wow, that's a new dress. Rather tight but sexy. Didn't know you liked these kinds of dresses". He was right. He is naturally configured not to notice women dresses unless they are glaringly attention seeking. Well, I had gained his attention.

Impression on me: he doesn't even notice my clothes anymore. I wear these dresses all the time.

Impression on him: what warrants that kind of a dress? Is there something I am missing? Do I need to be concerned? She does look sexy though.

Impression on you: Diverting some. Let's get back on track.

Dealing with Family: If I say painful, will you hate me?

Again, controlling the cynical side of me. Families are a blessing when you have mastered the art of not letting them enter your head. Families are made of people. People will talk. But when family members talk, by the sheer nature off the DNA configuration, those words tend to get into your ear and your head. Some very smart individuals learn how to tune those frequencies out in the short term. But it takes a very enlightened person to tune out those frequencies forever. If you are one of those, I have a huge amount of respect for you. You have mastered the art of cleansing your mind and soul of noise. Kudos to you.

If you recall, my two cents during the part about honeymoon. You had constructed a cocoon for yourself and your love. Stay in that cocoon for as long as you can. The reason you went away was you were creating a life size noise cancelling situation. Now, the noise is going to be nearby, a walk, a drive, a flight or a phone call away. How do you manage that?

Have your family time. And then wrap it up. Once that family time is done, put it behind you and forget about it. It was great when you had your and your life-partner's family around. Now they have left. Expunge all the noise. Don't worry about it. Do you think you can do that? I would advise, try not to explore, analyze or over think about what was said or not said when you had them over or when you visited them. Try to think about only the fun and good stuff. Don't think about the look that you saw your aunt was giving your spouse or the off-handed remark your dad made about the food served by your spouse. People talk. Fortunately or unfortunately, people are designed to be talkers without realizing the long term consequences of their words. But as you think about your life with another person, a person very dear to you, think beyond words. At least try.

A recommendation I have is to actually use words to negate words. After visiting relatives, find peace by using your words such that your ears can hear them. Tell yourself and your life-partner that you are now taking a deep breath. Please know that not all encounters with families are going to leave you feeling sapped and drained. Not every encounter is going to be negative. Not every encounter is going to need this advice. It is for those encounters that have the slightest potential of turning the course as it did in my marriage.

Families (both his and mine) had been a sore point of contention. Our families couldn't be more different. And that made a whole lot of difference to us. For reasons unknown. Being twelve years older and twelve years wiser than when I started my nuptial relationship, I can safely say, who the bloody hell should have cared? Did it matter that his family struggled to live within smaller means while mine had a more exuberant life style. Did it matter that they appreciated the more traditional cuisines while mine loved to experiment. Did it matter that when they ate, there was usually an umbrella of silence while when mine got together, the neighbors complained of how loud the laughter was.

It mattered then. I had entered a family that was so different than mine. They preferred different clothes, different style of eating, different family customs, and different style of speaking. And it was important for my ex. It was important that I become a part of that fabric. Just as it was important for me to know that he liked my family fabric. It mattered enough that when we had family gatherings and I sat on the side quietly, he didn't like it. He wanted me to participate. I wanted him to participate too. But he didn't want to because there was an inherent friction between personalities. Natural. Different personalities.

But it is usually difficult to accept that sometimes, more often than not, different personalities don't usually mesh well together. You meet somebody on the road, have a few words, realize you don't really care to have any more and walk away. Well, families and relatives don't allow you that luxury. Whether you like or dislike, you have to accept and allow yourselves and them to have many more of those forsaken words. But why? Why was that important? One advice that I will share is that ultimately it shouldn't matter. Try and be more forgiving to your spouse than to yourself. When he/she is not ready to feel engaged in those family events, let be. It's really not that important and not life changing. Plan out family events such that you can spare your love the pain of having to be a hypocrite. I have a feeling you might gain more than lose in this battle. Your family and relatives are living their lives. They will notice the absence of your spouse and they will make snide comments. Learn to let go. Those comments are really not that important. You can actually make it your day. Be the hero for the day and turn the tables on everybody. Tell them that they need to do a better job of upping the ante on being a social magnet to keep the love of your life interested in attending these events.

The bottom line- understand what your priority is. If your priority is your love, your new life partner, let them know. And these small statements of openness and flexibility help solidify the marriage. Your spouse understands who is important. Your spouse appreciates that you have his/her back when the need arises.

Imagine the effect of you standing by your spouse even in his/her absence does to the relationship. It sends a strong message that others come later, they do first. It sends a strong message that you will be not entertaining others to be the noise between you and your love for this special person. But more than anything else, it sends a strong message to the world around you and the world you love about the love you hold for this relationship and for this special person. It is priceless.

Also, as a double whammy, your family and relatives know not to mess around with your own family. The family that you are now building. It is important to send that message. Remember how we are all ultimately animals. Animals don't have relatives and extended families to worry about. They have their mates and they take care of them. At least the big ones do.

Dependency: A necessary evil

This aspect is probably the most difficult one to explore in a marriage. The dependency factor. We all like to be taken care of. As children, we like that we depend on our parents, as young teenagers we depend on our friends, as young adults we are seeking the next person to fill the spot. Well, you filled the spot. But don't forget the dependency factor. What do you depend on your partner for? What is it that you either don't like doing or really can't that this other person fills the spot for?

I will share this experience that I had with a friend of mine. Her husband was a successful executive with an excellent firm and climbing the ladders of Corporate America. Right after marriage, she tried her hands with a small time job. Then had babies and decided to step back into the home field. That kept her busy. She was happy. But they weren't. He was busy. He was travelling. He had a wonderful wife and a beautiful home. But he showed want of something. Something definable. He wanted to be challenged and excited at home. In his mind he had a beautiful home and a wonderful wife but somebody who would just do what he wanted. She will go a mile for him but that's not all that he wanted. He actually wanted somebody who would be an alternate earner in the household. He wanted somebody who would walk in high heels and tight skirts, share a drink when they both return from their work and share their work ideas. Here is what he didn't realize or accept; she always wanted to be a home maker. She wanted to stay at home, make it pretty, she wanted to be at home when he returned tired and take care of him.

When they had tied themselves in their "I do" join, they knew their parts in that union. One earned (more than the other); the other managed some other aspects like home making and child bearing. The balance was created. But somewhere, there was a breakdown in that understanding. She wanted to solely build the home and he wanted to climb that success ladder which in turn required somebody to keep the anchor at home (her). That's where the balance broke down.

What he didn't realize was that the balance was actually aligned. He couldn't be successful in his career and have his two sons taken care of how he wanted if she didn't keep the anchor at home. What she didn't realize was that she couldn't only be the perfect home maker if that home wasn't funded and paid for. They had a mutual dependency. They just needed to say it to each other.

In my very humble opinion, mutual dependency is probably the most important ingredient in marriage. Understand I didn't say love or passion. I say marriage. There has to be a void that your partner fulfils for you. A void that you need to be filled. For my friends it was the anchor at home and the provider voids.

So, what happens to the couples who are in double income families? I was in one of them. The dependency for provisions becomes less. I could earn, so could my ex. What we needed was not the financial support. What we needed was the partnership. If both careers are equally important, I have to admit, the tides get rough. It is a balance that gets misaligned more often. But if the weighing scale is stacked such that one side is happy being slightly lesser than the other, the balance can be tied very well.

I like to think of this dynamic like a weighing scale. Stack up what you bring to the marriage and ask your spouse to do the same. It's even better when you speak about it. Many couples suffer from not speaking out their thoughts. We think but we hesitate to talk. I always wonder why till I realized that I started speaking much later in the marriage; a bit too late. If I had started speaking unorthodox thoughts from the get go, I wouldn't have surprised my spouse when I did start speaking. And by then it wouldn't have sounded unorthodox either. Speaking about such things is considered calculated, sounds clinical. But let's agree it's better to be clinical and transparent versus having dirt thrown in later on.

Imagine my friends having this conversation; I will keep the home; and I will spend a lot of time making sure we are well fed and well kept. You can choose the words. But what is wrong with just saying those things aloud. At least you are clear. While dating, you would have learned about the other person and you think you know what each of you want from the marriage. But once you actually become one unit, one family, expectations might change. A miraculous change usually happens when kids come along. They seem to have a wonderful effect on people.

Try speaking your mind clearly, openly and vocally. Let your partner know what you want from the marriage. Let your partner know what the dependency you would like to have. And don't make the mistake of expecting your spouse to be a mind reader. You are not and neither are they. How about verbalizing what you want. This should be considered courtesy to the marriage and the partner you have chosen to spend the rest of your life with.

YOUR time: Protect it.

Find time for yourself and just for yourself. Spend it how you want. Spend that quality time which is for nobody but you. It is precious. Families and marriages have a tendency of sucking you in. You are married, you have a home, you are decorating, you are making new friends, you are busy getting accepted and acclimatized with your new family-in-law. You are busy. You soon forget yourself. Soon you are twenty pounds heavier. Soon you would have forgotten who you were and what you used to be. That is just wrong. Wrong for you and wrong for the marriage.

Remember that your spouse had liked what he saw in you. You had your personality, your likes, your dislikes, your wishes, dreams, wants, desires, carefreeness and idiosyncrasies. They were liked. Your spouse bought into the whole package. Why forget about the package to create a new one?

More than being unjust to you, it is a big mistake for the marriage. Forgetting about your individuality in the marriage is a lethal mistake. Two individuals come together in the holy realms of matrimony. Their individualities don't vanish. One should sustain theirs and help enhance their partners.

Taking time out to keep you rooted to your wishes and dreams is extremely important. I loved music. I heard music while going to sleep and woke up with my fingers reaching for the button on the music plyer. My music was very different from what my ex liked. I would share my music with him and he did the same with me. During the initial days, we tried liking each other's. But that desire to like music that I really did not like went away slowly. Along with that went my desire to find time to listen to mine. Don't know why but other things took priority. Work, home, lunches, dinners etc. But music was extremely important and I forgot about that. A part of me was now trapped, waiting for release. Only the music world was changing and I hadn't kept up with my genre. Result: when I did try to listen and tune back in, I was lost. Didn't recognize singers, lyrics, music, style anything. Hence I entered into that vortex of cyclical reasoning. I don't know the current music, so I don't listen. And because I don't listen, I don't know the current music. It took my seven year old son's interests and my baby sister's constant pounding about music that finally got me back into the thick of things.

I have heard so many similar stories. Keeping yourself hooked onto things you like is important for your growth within and outside the marriage. If you like to exercise or run, bike, sing, write, sketch, mix music or simply read books, do find time to do that. Even if you think you don't need it, your spouse does. That time allows him/her to go and do what they like.

Also, taking time out to take care of you is also important. It is a reflection of how you feel about yourself. If you still feel the way you did when you walked down that aisle, imagine that everyday could be your special day. Many people think once they enter their nuptial bliss, they can be easy on themselves. Keeping yourself feeling fit and fine is very important for your mental makeup. You are the only one to define what the fit and fine looks like. Nobody can tell you that. Or they shouldn't.

I liked being approximately hundred pounds in weight with a slim waste. I reflect that in the way I talk, the way I walk, how I present myself and how I feel. It also got reflected on what I wore. Smarter clothes made me feel happier and classier. As I started putting on weight, I would start wearing clothes that just didn't fit as well. And then it was that vortex again whereby I would reason that I didn't wear the right clothes because I felt heavy and I felt heavy because I didn't wear nice clothes. Women and their thoughts/ analysis can be so overwhelming!

Taking care of how you look and how you take care of yourself tells a story to your partner. That you still care of what they thought. You still wanted to look your best for them to admire. You still considered it important to feel sexy and desirable. You keep the heat on in the relationship. That goes both ways though. Hopefully, your spouse does you the same honor. It is important for the relationship.

When you have the love of your life, look like the dreamboat you wanted to spend the rest of your life with, you end up spending the rest of your life with them. The fire is still alive, the passion still burning, the lust ignited and life is good.

Bottom line- don't give up on yourself just because you are now domesticated. Keep the package that was once liked, still likable.

Also, taking time to do things that groom you is equally important. Taking the time out for your hair appointment, your nails, your spa, your messages, your golf or tennis is very important. That's the 'me' time when you are doing something to tell yourself, I am valuable. You are sending the strong message, I deserve things. Those who give up end up not getting them either.

If you send the signal to your spouse that your nails are no longer that important, your hair can be tied in a pony, your golf lessons have diminished in value, and your spouse will probably accept it just as it is. They don't want to make you do things. You don't like that. They want you do to what you want to do. Apparently, now you don't want beautiful nails, hair, sexy golf clothes or tennis rackets. You didn't ask, so you didn't get.

On the other hand, if you exhibit that all YOUR activities are important; your spouse will register accordingly. You get because you asked. Since you got you know your spouse cares and that keeps him/her in good graces.

Your space: is important!

What do you mean by your space? Your space is when you need that breathing room. Many a times, you get into the habit of explaining and expressing your every action and activity to your spouse. You are going to the mall with friends, you are running out for grocery, you are heading out for a round of golf, you are heading out for dinner with your business associates etc. etc.

Do you remember the time, you were dating? You were doing stuff with your now partner, but you were also doing things by yourself. You HAD things to do by yourself. And do you know what it resulted in? Your partner knew where you were but also where you weren't. That created a little bit of anxiety, a little bit of angst, a little bit of sweet tension and a little bit of questioning. It actually resulted in the two of you thinking about each other at times when you didn't need to. Guess what, that was kind of fun. Admit it. You wanted to know what your girlfriend or boyfriend was doing at a time when he/she just was doing their stuff. You wanted to know. You thought about it. You wondered if your love was thinking about you during those times away.

Why do you want to give it away? Giving too much information sometimes becomes somewhat predictable! Yes, hard to believe and very hard to accept this as a fact when somebody is trying to train you to see how marriage can work. But the idea is not to create the known and the predictability. The idea is to keep the exotic tension that the two of you shared once, alive. Remember tension (imagine a rope being pulled in different directions) is when forces are running in opposite directions, but when you release that tension, the two opposite ends collapse into the same sphere of togetherness. On the floor...in a heap.

All I advise is keep the unspoken tension alive. Go away and do you things. I am not asking you to go and have affairs. Please, goodness NO! On the contrary, do what gives you space from that togetherness, such that when you do have that precious togetherness, you realize how precious it is. Nothing is predictable except for the breathing, eating and sleeping. The rest is slightly unknown, slightly exotic, slightly guessed and slightly unpredictable.

Imagine yourself as the beautiful, exotic home-maker. Your spouse has gone out to earn the beautiful green to make things happen for the two of you. You are done with planning for dinner and the weekend party. You have time. Head out to watch a movie or have drinks.

Many folks will drop a text or a voice mail (we now call it touching base) with your love. You want to let him/her know where you will be. You sign off by saying "I love you". That is sweet and precious. But does your spouse really want to know where you are going to be? If they do, does it need to be right before you go? How about afterwards, over dinner, when you get asked? A nice dinner statement that says you were busy. Busy in your own space.

The word I am seeking is crowded. It can feel like a crowd sometimes even with two people in it. You get to know each other. You know each other's moves, habits, thoughts etc. It seems wonderful when it starts since you are in the learning mode. You are absorbing information through actions, activities, patterns and words shared between the two of you. But soon it becomes ... yes, predictable. You get the text, but scan through it versus really reading it. You know that you are getting the same "Hey, I am just stepping out for a little bit to get the last minute stuff for the party on Saturday", "Hi, just wanted to let you know that the mowers came in late but asked them to take down the trees, just like we discussed last night". You will get the feel soon enough.

Try this for a change. How about putting a little space, maybe an hour of daily activities, between you and your love. You go do your thing and let him/her do theirs. You touch base often with an "xxx", "muah" or a "xoxo". Touch base with a "Hey- all ok?" or "Hey- Just wanted to say last night was ....."

That puts a smile on a special face when facing assholes in a meeting. That tells that special someone that somebody is waiting for them and that the world outside the meeting room is more meaningful. But just enough information to evoke the questions. Just enough to start a conversation versus a dump of information.

You gave your partner space and in turn got yours. Here is something that usually happens in many to most marriages as years keep rolling by. You start crowding each other's space. You make things very easy to decipher. The fun goes away. The excitement diminishes. Why do you want to risk it? Try and sustain that fun. Keep it a little unknown.

Mankind always gets intrigued by the unknown. Mankind likes unpredictability. They like solving that predictability to set patterns. You and your partner are going to do the same. But once that unpredictability is solved, and then things become somewhat "normal". And guess what, we as humans don't like "normal".

Try not to make things "normal" and "boring" for your relationship. Try and make it exotic, erotic and tantalizing. Try and make it scintillating. Whatever rocks your world?

You shouldn't get married and think that now it's all about everything that you do together. Do things separately, such that there is mutual learning. But also this keeps you in your partner's mind just like it used to be during your courtship period. Guess what I am trying to get at is don't give up on your courtship period. Keep the same energy and same excitement for as long as you can. And keeping your personal space is an important ingredient for that success.

Also, recall that man is after all an animal. Animals evolve. We are also evolving as people. We are morphing with changing wants, desires, wishes and personality. Let that happen naturally.

But this is a truly slippery slope. I will be honest. If you don't start from the get go, you might create the inertia of your spouse expecting you to be predictable. When you suddenly start carving out that space for yourself later, your spouse will sniff a different message. This will play havoc on their mind and your relationship. The very natural thoughts to germinate are those of infidelity. "Is there another person now", "Why this sudden change in behavior", "Is there something fishy going on now". Very natural thoughts for a normal human being.

Again talking about it right off the bat is always helpful. But if you can't talk, show. Exhibit that you are the person who needs space.

Just a little personal space to make sure you is evolving your individual personality as much as you are evolving in the relationship.

If you can talk, express your desire that you will want to not disturb your love during the day. You want to make sure that you are both doing what makes you happy. Tell your love how much you love him/her. But keep those dating days alive. Nourish it. It will help you in the long run.

Now think about not the day but a longer time frame. How about going out for a vacation with your school friends or your siblings? You going out on your own are not an insult to your spouse's visions of wanting to take you on your next vacation. Just carve time out which is separate from that romantic vacation. Don't hold yourself back. Don't slash down your wishes just because they are not completely aligned with your spouses. You do that once, you do that twice, but soon you start to regret and get frustrated. You ultimately take it out on the relationship. You feel like you are trapped.

Don't subject your poor spouse to that because of choices you are making right now. You do have a choice of expressing yourself and your desires. You spouse will understand when you state it like that. Somebody who loves you will see that you have the fire in you to do things in life as an individual. Somebody who loves you will see you need your space.

I have a feeling you will realize that the going away will in turn help your relationship. Some smart person once said - "Absence makes the heart grow fonder". It is a very true saying. Some slight short timed distance actually does help the heart grow fonder.

When you step out of that space, you put more value and perspective to the space that you share with your love. You realize that there is a different kind of feeling in being in that cocooned space with somebody who is special. The analogy that I draw is light. Try staring at the sun for long. Soon that light begins to seem like darkness. You can't see anything. Your natural instinct is to turn away. You look away into a space which has less glaring light or even darkness. But when you turn back to look into the light, your vision is clearer. You can see the light again. See it for what it is.

Getting your space helps you and it helps your spouse.

Your mental harmony: is chaotic.

There is always a pattern to chaos and clarity in the chaotic. We focus so much on the chaos and the chaotic that we forget to seek the pattern and the clarity.

Who are you? What do you like? What gives you peace? And once you find the peace, how do you value it?

Let me get your brain cells going.

Problem solving gives me mental harmony. It gives me a sense of purpose and achievement.

I like to be challenged. I love working.

How do I recognize it? Through recognition and rewards.

Once achieved, I find value in using the experience to seek out the next mountain to climb or problem to be solved.

I am like a mechanism that just wants to keep going on.

That's who I am today. I can promise you this that in another ten years' time; I will not be giving that same answer. I would have evolved and would be a slightly different person with some revised wants and wishes.

If you can't truly define who you are today, how can you expect another person, no matter how close they are to you, to have the answer for you? But marriage has another well-known factor. You tend to think your spouse can read your mind. Men claim they can't understand what women want. Women claim that men are insensitive to everything but themselves.

Both claims are right and wrong at some level. When mankind came to earth, they didn't get parceled here with a book that spoke about marriage. They were animals. They hunted for food, found shelter to stay in, protected themselves from bigger predators and when they had carnal desires, they had sex. Sexual desires are natural but marriage is manmade. Men designed the institution of marriage to bring some harmony to the chaos that had started somewhere in history. Having a certificate that claimed exclusivity of your partner was something that other (some wise) men structured to ensure that human kind realized that it's not free for all like other animal species.

As we evolved in our thinking, we started refining the institute. Slowly we started bringing the aspects of expectation into this institution. And all these evolving aspects of marriage have now conditioned it. People walking into a marriage are expecting certain things.

I tend to disagree with many of the normal expectations from marriage. It might help many but those who tell you that they walk through married life without thinking "what the hell have I done",

"Is this what life holds for me for the rest of it", "I have to stand by this marriage and show my commitment", are either kidding you or themselves. Thoughts arise. When you have to think that this is a commitment that you HAVE to show consistency to, you are doing your marriage and your spouse an injustice. It shouldn't be anything you HAVE to do. You didn't HAVE to walk down the aisle. You definitely didn't HAVE to say yes to the proposal. You didn't HAVE to propose in the first place.

But you did because you want. Staying true to that "I want to" aspect of you is extremely important. It then brings out the best of you to everything that you do in your marriage. It is not easy. I understand that. I know because I failed to do so myself. But if only I had stood by my truth and my true feelings to myself first, it would have been reflected in my feelings towards my spouse. Marriage is just a certification for the society to know that you are going to stay exclusively committed to that one person. Remember the vow... "Till death do us part". Your commitment to the love of your life doesn't require a certification. It should be evident. It should be felt, not written down.

If you truly want to be yourself in the marriage, take some time to think about your mental harmony. What is important to you?

Once you have found a true outline of that mental harmony, how about sharing it with your love? Tell your spouse about what gives you peace and happiness. You two are two different individuals. You don't have to feel shy or afraid of sharing those thoughts with your love. He/she has accepted you for who you are. They will love you for who you are. Not because you reminded them of their parents or it felt like you will be a great person to have stability in the house and hopefully definitely not for you being a good provider. Hopefully, you all decided to share life together because you liked who your spouse was and they in turn like who you are.

Imagine that you actually love the aspect of making money. Not because of things that you can buy or big houses that you can live in. You like making money, to feel secure. You never want to feel helpless about anything in life anymore. You want to work hard to get that money. The journey of working hard to achieve this simple goal gives you a thrill. Share it. Share it with your spouse. Tell her/him how important it is to you. Let them into your inner most thoughts. Be vulnerable with your partner of choice. What that achieves is that now your partner knows why you go an additional mile above and beyond your call of duty to make sure you shine out in office. You might miss a few home duties but want to make sure that nothing slips through the cracks when it comes to your commitment to your job or the job that you have your eye set on. Your partner will help make that happen. He/she loves you. He/she knows that if this aspect of your life gives you happiness, you will be a happier person coming back home into your personal cocoon.

On the other hand, imagine that you don't like the simplicity of love making. You like it exotic, you like it erotic, and you like it sudden and unexpected. Share it. Share it with the one person hopefully who has every right to know that. There is no shame in liking a certain way of expressing your carnal innermost desires. Remember that's natural. Everything else in marriage is manmade. Express yourself. If you like out of the ordinary aspects of sex, let your partner know, if they don't already know.

You must be wondering why is letting them know important. "They should know since we have dated before the marriage. They will of course know the transparent happenings of a bedroom." You might be more surprised than not at how often two people who are madly in love, don't share their deepest darkest thoughts and desires. Reason, they don't want to risk losing the one person they love so much for something that society has deemed to be dark in the first place. We can celebrate our marriage with 500 people around us but sex (the most natural aspect of life) is a scintillating, secretive and often taboo topic to talk about. People blush at this topic which means they are either embarrassed or flushed at the thought of it.

Just taking this as an example, have you spoken about your inner most desires with your partner? Have you shared the kind of experiences you have had in previous life (before having met this very special person) with him/her? You probably had experimented then with different Kamasutra style postures or flirtations. You had liked them. They made you realize the true animal side of you. They were a part of you. Have you had the courage to share these thoughts with the person you will be spending the rest of your life and bed with? Most people don't do that for several reasons. What will they think? It will expose that you had multiple partners before him/her (a societal no no). It will bring some sort of insecurity in the mind of your partner. You might even be embarrassed about the things that you like. You don't want your love to recognize that carnal side of you.

Everything you have thought about this aspect (as stated above) makes perfect sense. But it doesn't make perfect sense when you have to hide your true self from the person who means so much to you. They love you, no matter what. That entails loving you, or at least recognizing you for who you truly are. If they don't want to

81

participate in that kind of sexual endeavor, that's understandable and appreciable. But at least there is now transparency in the relationship. You now know where they stand and they, in turn, know where you do.

Here is what might happen if you don't share. Those thoughts and desires are a part of you and your personality, whether you like it or not. They make you who you truly are. So big deal if you like dirty stuff (hopefully to a dignified limit). You have also exhibited to your partner that you are ready to reign in those thoughts and desires for the sake of your love. The special person has already been given priority over your thoughts and desires. But if you don't share, those thoughts are not going away. They are hiding somewhere inside you. Later in life, when things are dull and boring (and they do get dull and boring at different parts of life about different aspects of life), you will seek to fulfil this side of your desires somehow. Sometimes, in extreme cases, they manifest themselves in extra-marital affairs. Why risk it? When you know what your partner likes and he/she knows what you like, when things get dull and boring, maybe you can find ways to pull these thoughts and desires into your life (in whatever way you all are comfortable with). But at least your partner and you know what those thoughts are. Ignorance can lead to dangerous grounds. Again, why risk it?

You are risking that these vulnerabilities might come back to bite you when you are getting into conflict stages at different parts of your married life though. This risk also needs to be defined such that you make an educated decision about sharing as well. Too much sharing or too many details might lead to dangerous grounds as well.

Hopefully, as you are thinking or "getting trained" for marriage, you already are aware that conflict is that sweet little monster that nobody mentions right now, but is very much a part of life. You can hide from it but it's a reality of life. Every relationship goes through conflict stages. In ways, it also strengthens your relationship.

As you have your disagreements, you tend to forget rationale thoughts. You are hurt and you sometimes intend to hurt the other person. (If you don't do these things, you should be training me on conflict management). But in hurting the other person, especially if this person is close to your heart and identity, you will know where to hurt and what to hurt with. You will pick from your memory bank all those vulnerabilities to be used for that "fight". Don't worry; it is normal human nature. But also don't fool yourself in thinking that you are far too dignified to do so. And another aspect worth mentioning; if you don't have conflict or "fights" or disagreements, please visit a marriage counsel. That also means that you and your spouse have stopped feeling in this relationship. It has become very mechanical now. But if you do have a normal relation, you have your occasional disagreements and you are brutal. You will pick and choose everything that your spouse has shared with you in confidence and use them. And trust me, your spouse will return the favors. Remember, when these "fights" take place, your intention then turns from rational thought process to irrational feelings. You, most probably, in the heat of the moment, want to hurt. You have been hurt. You will choose whatever weapon comes your way. And in sharing and being transparent, each of you have given the other person, plenty of ammunition to work with.

Be careful. Don't do that. Try not to bring those innermost thoughts and desires into the "fights". That can have long lasting impact that you really don't want. Let some vulnerabilities remain. Let's leave this for now and we will visit this later in another chapter.

Your happiness: is YOUR responsibility!

You get into beautiful relationship thinking now you are handing over the baton of your happiness in the hands of your partner. He/she will make you happy. In turn, your sole intention is to make him/her happy. Excellent idea but very poor chance of success.

How many times have you heard people say "nobody knows what women want" or "Men are impossible to understand". That clearly states that neither man nor woman is really decipherable or understandable. If it had been so easy, smart engineers (who have now designed human robots) would have been able to program thoughts, feeling and emotions into humans as well. That aspect remains absent from design because they are impossible for mankind to fully comprehend and decipher.

So, in essence, we don't know how happiness is measured or defined by the other person. How about defining our own happiness? Can you clearly state what makes you happy? Many of you will say yes. But those same many of you will be unable to keep that list consistent for the rest of your life. What makes you happy now will probably not make you happy ten years from now. So, why do you want to burden your spouse with the responsibility of holding this ever changing list, when you yourself find it difficult to keep that list solidly engraved in your head? That doesn't seem fair. But that's how society has defined marital responsibility. Even when taking vows, you will promise that you will try to make the other person happy. Well, don't make empty promises. What we should in turn be saying is "I will try to ensure that whatever makes you happy is important to me".

Your happiness is truly your responsibility. And one aspect of life that I have learned is that unless you are a happy person, you can forget about trying to make anybody around you happy. It's a simple fact of life that people just simply can't grasp or comprehend.

Does being a valued home maker with full throttle energy for your kids' school, PTA, holding envy inducing parties at home, having the ability to change the décor of your home with every season and looking your stunning self, make your happy? Or does the adrenalin rush of driving your career to dizzying heights, making decision worth millions of dollars, running pillar to post to ensure that when in retirement, you will hold a net worth of millions; make you happy? Or does making exotic meals that create the talk of the town, being charitable and philanthropic with your time and money, making others smile and giving to others, make your happy?

Don't worry; I like you, found it really hard to define what truly makes me happy. And what was even more difficult was to succinctly put it into two to three sentences. It is difficult to state something for yourself. But once you have succeeded in truthfully stating that list, you will see how easy it is to make it happen (assuming you have the right skill sets to do so). This last aspect brings a smile to my face. Here is the reason why.

Making money and being challenged in my career, makes me happy. But on my less complicated side, having the exotically decorated home (clean, well-kept and looked after) makes me happy. I tried for many years to make both happen by myself. I would work like crazy in office and then come home and start cleaning, turning décor around, researching the next style that the home should be in. I drove myself nuts! I was so unhappy at home. Nothing seemed to fit. I didn't like the results at all. Till I realized I am not a great home maker. I might be a designer by training from a previous life, but horrible at my own home making. I could do it for others but couldn't satisfy myself when it came to my dream home. I had the right aspirations for happiness but lacked the true skill set to make it happen. But someone else did. I just had to find that one person. I was good in office. So I focused there. I focused on making myself happy in office to earn the green bucks to then come home and hire a designer, give them my vision and let them make it happen for me. Nowhere had I stated that I wanted the dream home that I would put together. I just needed the home for me to walk into.

Clearing your head to state clearly what makes you happy also makes it easier to define how you can make it happen for yourself. Does it make you think I am training you to be selfish? In a peculiar sort of way, I am. In some sort of selfless way, you want to be happy to make others around you happy. How many times have you looked around you and found people who seem just very unhappy. And how many times have you said to yourself, "I so badly want to hang around with this unhappy person". Hopefully not too many times, unless you are attracted to negativity (Yes, there are some who like that sort of thing). People usually don't want to hang around unhappy people. Why would you want to subject your loved ones to that? If you are happy, you will know how to make others happy.

Sometimes, making yourself happy might seem disruptive or strange to your spouse. Playing golf every Sunday helps relax you and keeps that smile. But Sunday is when you and your spouse also have many of your social engagements that he/she anxiously wants to entertain. Manage the situation. How about your tee off really early morn, such that you come back by afternoon to head out for your social engagements. Or let him/her do what they want to do independently. Don't let society dictate that you always have to keep those social engagements together. If one of you can check the box on them while you find your true happiness, what is wrong with that scene?

When you are true to your spouse by telling him/her about your true thoughts (not affected by emotions or adulterated by other motives); your spouse will appreciate that. They don't want to see you miserable. They want that smile because that's what makes them smile. Smiles can be very inductive. We don't use enough of them. If your spouse realizes that playing golf, while missing that lunch appointment at Aunt Haggard's place, will mean you all will be smiling and laughing during dinner time and thereafter, who wouldn't sign up for that? On the alternative, dragging you to that wonderful lunch while all you could think of how you could have worked on that left swing on course 7 will only create silence during dinner. Or worse... noise that you can do without. Noise in your head. Keep it simple, keep it clean.

Imagine the contrary. You are feeling low and sad. You wear that look that screams "leave me alone". With that state of mind, you accompany your spouse over to your Aunt Haggard's for lunch on that beautiful Sunday. Everybody is rejoicing and talking vociferously. Nobody is "leaving you alone". You keep feeling this burning lava inside. You desperately want to get out to the back yard to find some quiet time. But every time you do that, somebody comes over to have small talk with you about your golf game these days or about how your job is going. Again, NOBODY is LEAVING YOU ALONE! That burning lava keeps boiling inside till it finds a vent. And that vent will come. It will surface. And when it does, it will not be pleasant.

Save yourself and your spouse the journey to the center of your angry self. Please! You are having a bad day, you want to be left alone, and you want some quiet time. Let your spouse know in those exact terms. Ask her/him to help you find a way such that you all don't have to subject yourself to the negative energy turning into that hot lava. Your spouse might be able to help you out. A suggestion like "Look, I can manage Aunt Haggard today. Why don't you get into PJ's and chill in bed with a couple of beers and a movie?" Or... "To hell with Aunt Haggard! We will make some excuse. I don't want to go without you and don't want to go with you feeling this way. Why don't we just chill in the swimming pool and take a few laps". Or "Why don't you go do what you need to do, don't worry about this at all today?"

All you had to do was reach out for happiness and reach out with honest words to your spouse. That's all that it takes. They don't want to make you miserable. On the contrary, they want that smile and the genuine happiness. Because selfishly, they also want to be happy. Everybody wants to be happy. They mire their simple wants with thoughts like "I don't want to hurt her feelings" or "I don't want to put my wife/husband through the social embarrassment. It means a lot to her". Do your own thinking. Spare your spouse the punishment by not thinking for him/her. They are very capable of doing their own thinking. You just need to verbalize your own thoughts, wishes and wants.

Happiness also means simplicity. You might find happiness in complex and complicated things. Frankly, as hard as I find to comprehend, some people might find utter and exhilarating happiness in complex differential mathematical equations or computer coding five hundred pages long. Hey, to each his own. But I find life's happiness very easy and in simple statements. The rest is the garnishing that comes with it.

Being rich makes me happy.

Being close to my siblings make me happy.

Playing with my kids make me happy.

Being challenged at work makes me happy.

Being outdoors makes me happy.

Being in a big city makes me happy.

Being in a small city with my friends and family close by makes me happy.

Writing makes me happy.

Sports make me happy.

Travel makes me happy.

It's these small statements, simple and succinct, now makes me happy. They are definable. They are doable. They are now achievable.

Once I was asked, what makes you happy? I was going through a terrible phase in my life where frankly, nothing was making me happy. My response was "Travelling makes me happy". My friend went on to ask "What about travel makes you happy?" Stupid question, right? But I didn't want to insult her. So I went on to say, "Airport, seeing other people, getting into the airplane, watching movies, being fed food while flying, the takeoff, the landing and meeting complete strangers whom I probably won't meet ever

SOMEBODY... Train me for MARRIAGE!

again, makes me happy." I probably failed to mention that she (yes, a woman) was persistent to the point of being nagging. She kept at it. Relentlessly. "So you like the commute part, not necessarily the destination. No where did you mention London, Tokyo, New York or New Delhi. So, what do you like when you are at the airport or in the plane itself?" A pain in the backside is the first thought that ran through my head. Patiently though I pondered over her statements and questions. Truth be told, I actually don't think about the destinations, only about the fact that I am traveling. So, what was it that I liked about it being at the airport or the plane? "At the airport, I watch people walk by. Complete strangers but so many of them all around you. Yet, you don't know most. Everybody is going somewhere. But I really like being in the plane. The fact that I am helpless. I can't get up and walk away. I am held captive in that box of metal where I can shut the rest of the world out legitimately. It gives me peace." She smiled and sat back. And I felt like a complete arse. She had to dig it out of me but "Being left alone in my own cocoon makes me happy". Being the busy person that I am, I wanted to find myself in that solitude. I wanted to give my brain some peace. That's all I needed to say to her. But I probably used every alphabet allowed to   get   to   that.

Your happiness is very simple. It is very straight forward. We just manage to make a huge mess of it. Especially in explaining it to ourselves.

Being in the state of mind that I was in, I was finding happiness in being left alone even if I was in a crowd. I wanted to feel quiet. But I didn't define it for myself. I was seeking travel to find it. I loved the sixteen hour flights to Tokyo from Chicago to elongate the time I could be in that cocoon. I didn't need to travel for that. I just needed to define it for my spouse in those simple terms that I was feeling bad about circumstances and being the sharp minded intellectually stimulated type "A" personality that I am, I would like to be left alone for some time. He would have respected me saying this in those simple terms to him. Instead, I chose to run away from home to find that solitude, which caused more damage to my marriage than help. All he could see was I was travelling and didn't want to talk about it at all. Well, frankly I didn't want to talk. My brain and my mind wanted to reboot. Simple. I didn't want to shut him out. I just needed him to know that I was going into shut down mode for some time.

Somewhere in our lives, we forget to find simplicity. Try to seek that simplicity of words stating what makes you truly happy. Convey it to your loved one. I am sure they can do the same.

Then you can start looking at the path forward to make that happiness into reality.

Another thing to remember is that factors that make you happy today will not remain constant. As you grow, as you get exposed to different aspects of life, your happiness factor will change. It is bound to happen. So don't be hard on yourself and your spouse on changing factors that can make you happy.

Suppose you have done the most amazing thing. You discovered for yourself what makes you happy, you vocalized them to your spouse and you started putting them into action. Five years down the lane, you realize that now there are other things and actions that make you happy. You now state them to your spouse. Imagine the chaos you are creating for your lives. The very natural reaction for your spouse is going to be "What the hell? We put in all the effort into making you happy and now you tell me that you don't want this but something else?"

Yes, that is bound to happen, BUT only if you don't manage it well. First recognize that you and your emotions are evolving. Don't be hard on yourself and please don't be hard on your spouse. Plans change. We change. It is as natural as breathing and sleeping. You need to change or else you will stagnate and fossilize. (Ok, that's a bit harsh and extreme but you get the point).

Allow yourself to be honest. Don't accept that things that you had stated made you happy ten years back, should be the same things that make you happy today. You probably have met more people, seen many more things, and learned a ton more and realized that there are many more things to life. Or you could have achieved some of those goals that you set out for happiness and now you want to expand your vision.

Your spouse will react (especially if he/she has worked very hard to make sure that the two of you as individuals are happy). But when they calm down, they will realize that it's better to be honest with each other about such things. What would you rather have; working towards a plan that one of you knows is not really going to be called a success or re-thinking about the plan as adults and figuring out a new course of action. The common phrase used by married couples when they head down the divorce aisle is "we grew apart". You will grow. You can't stop that. But you can stop the 'apart' piece if you are honest and transparent about your feelings and thoughts with your spouse. Don't surprise them. Walk them as you walk yourself through this evolution. If not, you will risk one of you doing the catching up or inability to do so.

At one point in my life, travel made me happy. I wanted to see different places and meet different people. I did. But in meeting different people, seeing their achievements/failures, realizing that life has so much more to offer, my view of the world changed. I was now exposed to many more things that life and mankind has to offer than what my immediate current surrounding had placed in front of me. Suddenly, from being the satisfied, stable and conditioned individual I was, I wanted more. I wanted to, at least, give it a try and see if I could achieve some of those. But I kept my wants and wishes to myself. Why? Because I didn't want to come across as the bitch who keeps asking and seeking more. Never satisfied. Never content.

But couldn't hide my feelings that now I was unsatisfied. Those feelings got reflected in my behavior, my lack of appreciation for things around me, the negative comments about my surroundings and general unhappiness.

The one person, who was the first to notice this change in me, was my spouse. He knew that somehow I wanted something other than what we had and what we had been working for. Even though the realization came, the actions didn't. No matter how much we think of our spouses to be God-send, they are after all human. He just saw my current state of mind as being dissatisfied. With what and why were really not that important because I HAD NOT made it important. I had not verbalized in simple terms for myself and for him, that I wanted some other things in life now. Slightly expanded than what it was earlier. Nothing wrong with that statement, if stated in those simplistic terms. And nothing wrong with the statement if you view each other as mere humans who will have changing feelings and emotions instead of super-humans who should be the epitome of happiness.

Our spouses deserve the respect of being treated fairly. One just needs to be clear and vocal with them as much as we are with ourselves. If your happiness quotient is now changing, let them know. Also, let them know that you want to walk through this change with them. Otherwise, they start imagining the worst. Spouses have a tendency of taking a lot of blame on themselves and the relationship. The influencing factors might be completely external but we internalize it to have better control.

You got married, because you knew the importance of this other person in your life. This other person made you happy. Now your happiness quotient requires some other things outside the previously discussed aspects. Verbalize it for yourself and for your love. He/she deserves to know what is going on in your life. Together you can make things happen but they have to know what is happening in your mind before they can help. Don't make yourself miserable, because that's when you make the rest of your loved ones very unhappy. They need your genuine smiles, your laughter and openness more than the delicious food on the table or the well-manicured yards. They need the real YOU. And the real you need to be happy.

Doing things together: Necessary!

As much as I have discussed the need for individuality to be maintained in the marriage, it is also equally important to have some sort of bonds that tie you together outside of general day to day living.

The person you are married to is the one person who deserves to be given a chance to become your friend. A friend that you can confide in or feel vulnerable with. But not all married couples are friends. There is nothing wrong with giving that term to somebody other than your spouse. We didn't ask for best friendship status. We asked for enough transparency that at least there is a friendship status.

Now if you look back on your friends from childhood or adolescent life, you will think back on the movies you all watched, the games you all played, the books you shared and the laughter you all shared. Memories were created.

When we put our mind into the marriage framework, we automatically start thinking in very domesticated terms. The perfect home, the perfect kids (in the future), the perfect financial set up, the perfect vacations and the perfect life. But what about creating those memories outside of the gorgeous vacation, on a day to day basis?

What about doing things together where both of you get time to be not husband and wife, but just friends who are out to have fun. Like the time when you were dating, there were other activities that hopefully you engaged in.

Both of you liked movies and loved discussing and debating about the plot, the acting and direction. You used to take bike rides through the wilderness, hiked for hours in the quiet of the greens or swam hundred laps to see who finished first. Don't let those fantastic activities get lost now that you have to worry about mortgage, car payments, yard mowing or being the perfect hosts. Give those activities importance because that's when you are being just friends, pure unadulterated friends.

Doing things together with your spouse is very important to keep the marriage aerated. Now the normal question to ask is what if you didn't share any such activities together earlier but more random things, how do you build that into the pattern now? Fair.

Keep the random activities going on? Think back about what brought the "oomph" to your relationship. Was it the pub thrill, the night club experiences, the slightly flirtatious lunches, the surprise movie tickets that you appeared at their doorsteps with, or the

DVD's that you all enjoyed together? Think about the times when you felt the thrill and the utter relaxation of being in the company of your love. Keep that alive. Keep that going.

Marriage has a way of sneaking up on you. Before you know it, you will get sucked into living a "marriage" that others prescribe for you. Apologies for my French, but bull shit! Nobody defines your marriage. You and your love do. It is going to be the marriage you and your love want it to be.

A surprise lunch, a slow walk along the lake front, a few late night drinks, a random text about last night and the horrible cooking sessions that would leave the kitchen look like a war zone.

Sports have a wonderful way of tying people together without words. It's true for all humans but works wonders for couples. Imagine a friendly game of tennis or lap swimming. A little bit of competition, a little bit of win and loss, a little bit of flirtation and a lot of fun. The idea is not to win or the game itself. The idea is to have fun. The fun that is for the two of you.

You engage in these activities with friends. You engage in activities to let your guard down and just be yourself. You can do that with your spouse. Let him/her be a part of that silent thought process where the activity supersedes words.

These activities are considered stress relief and a mode to vent your (negative) energy. Imagine doing it with someone who can truly understand and stay connected. You can still relieve stress and vent but now your spouse knows what is going on in your mind. Not in words but in actions and through the attempt to control and mitigate it.

Why is it so important to have activities to engage in with your spouse? To stay engaged in activities outside the home. Simple. You had a life before you saw each other every day (if not every moment of your free life). You need to share some of that with your love. I think more importantly, it is important to feel like the single you and the single him/her before you were married. You need to keep that flavor alive when nothing else mattered and you enjoyed these moments during the day that you could spend with each other. So now you have a lot of these moments. You are together in one house. You have access to him/her whenever you want. But pretend that's not the case sometimes. Take that moment and go back to being your dating self.

The other important thing of not giving up on doing things together is that these are the things that are outside your marital boring stuff that you two still share.

Imagine now that your career has taken off and your spouse is flying high in his/her office. Your time is precious and you barely find time to slow down. What now?

Steal moments. It doesn't need to be every day. It doesn't need to regular, but find those moments to go back to those days when your dates were important. Find a couple of hours to zone the whole world out. Instead of discussing the next party that you have to attend or the next one to throw, drive out to the movies. Those parties will always stay and they will be there, even when you come out after watching Tom Cruise walks the walls of Mission Impossible. Or, instead of being the perfect household, order pizza and a whole bunch of DVD's that you will stay up the whole night with. Trash the house once in a while like you all did when nothing else mattered. You will get to clean it together again tomorrow. Again, steal the moments whenever possible and make them special. But do things together. And do it whenever possible. People talk of date nights and how special they are. And they are. But date nights are for once in a while. If you have the luxury of a little bit of time during the day, make every night a little date night in some way. You didn't need the restaurants or the fancy foods all the time before you were married. You just needed the little activities and little pleasures to share to make it special. Keep doing that.

Sustaining the feeling of being single in a marriage makes it special. Not because you still want to be. But because now you can have the freedom when you really don't want it. Yet the gentle reminder of that freedom with your spouse keeps an unspoken bond between the two.

Dealing with jealousy: Trust me, it's not going away!

You are a couple. Two different people who came together to stay united... That doesn't make this united front all sacrosanct. One or both of you will feel the quintessential stab of jealousy. Have the crawling feeling that somebody else has now entered this united front or at least can put a dent to the united front. One of you will think that the other is looking away because all is not great in the life that is now created for you.

What's so wrong with this picture? First, don't stab yourself for feeling this way. But more importantly, don't lose control over yourself because your spouse felt it. You are both human. You are bound to feel human emotions.

And remember we are still animals.

SOMEBODY... *Train me for MARRIAGE!*

Animals are territorial. They like their territory to be marked and respected. They don't want encroachment and they definitely show their displeasure when the marked territory is violated. They show their emotions.

So will you and your spouse. People interact. They react in certain ways to others. Both of you are out in the world dealing with others. It is very easy for one or both of you to feel that somebody else now has caught your attention or that there is a risk of that happening.

A very normal reaction that I used to let take over me when my spouse displayed any sense of jealousy was first to berate him. How could he feel this way? Does he not trust me enough? Does he not know me at all? Does he doubt me now? Does he not have faith in my commitment to the relationship? Does he doubt my commitment to him? All those were my feelings but what was wrong if he was. What he was feeling was a very normal human reaction to external factors and my reaction to them (or his perceived interpretation of my reaction to them). But I didn't marry a saint. I married a human. An animal.

Why was I expecting a different reaction? And what reaction would that be? Imagine the opposite. That he never felt jealous. He was ok with me being anyhow with whomever and he never brought it to my attention. Would it have given the signal that he doesn't care? Probably. There are those who never express jealousy. That's natural. But not feeling it is a different ball game. The expression might be subtle and for you to decipher but if a person feels for you, they will feel jealous. The hormones unfortunately work that way.

Now dealing with the jealousy is another thing. How do you deal with it? Do you nix your interaction with the other people concerned, do you change your behavior towards them, do you become conscious of how you behave with others in future such that your spouse doesn't have reason to feel this way. Some might say yes to all the above. I will vote for no.

Don't change yourself. Ask yourself. Maybe you are flirtatious; you use a little style in talking to some people. But also ask, is that just natural for you or is that with a particular person. If so, what is it that you are feeling? A little flirtation here and there is not harmful at all. Its normal human behavior. Very normal animal behavior.

But then ask yourself, if you have any interest in the other person. If the answer is yes, this is the wrong book for you right now. You have probably read enough. But you might want to be true to yourself and to your spouse.

But if the answer is no, then why worry? You enjoy an occasional flirtation but in your heart there is only one person who resides. And why would you want to change. You are who you are. If you are flirtatious, accept it. Flirtation is not harmful. Your spouse probably liked you for the exact same feature when he/she first met you. Asking you to change is neither fair nor useful. They should accept as you should that you are your own person but this person is fully committed to you. Feeling insecure about your personality is a problem that doesn't really have a solution. You can suppress or control your personality from surfacing in situations where you might feel you will give reason for your spouse to feel insecure. But that personality is not going away and in my humble opinion, suppressing it is being a hypocrite.

Imagine the tables turn. And you are the one who feels insecure. What will give you more peace? Knowing that your spouse listened to you and controlled his/her reaction to others or that they are free and open but you reside in their heart? I would choose the freedom of personality with the knowledge that I am the one whom that personality has chosen to walk life with.

This is a rather dangerous topic to discuss (leave aside train for). You have to train yourself but also train your spouse. And this is probably the first time I use "train your spouse" not "talk to your spouse". Here is why. First, you have to train yourself to be yourself. You are who you are. Don't go about making changes to your social personality because you don't want to create havoc at home. Of course, if you have a personality that exhibits less commitment to your vows, then think for yourself. But if you still stand by all your vows, then why would you change? You are who you are and that's the person who walked down the aisle.

Also, train yourself to stand by the same rules if you are the one to feel the pangs about your spouse. You can't expect your spouse to change all of a sudden only so you can sleep better knowing that you are the one.

Next you have to think about how to train your spouse's thinking about you. The jealousy requires externally focused actions. It actually requires the two of you to work towards the mutual security. If you ask your spouse to turnaround their personality, that will be injustice to him/her. On the same count, unfortunately, if your spouse requires you to change your personality to make them feel more secure and at peace, that will be injustice to you. To expect that such situations will not arise, will be foolhardy. So, best to be prepared and best to be honest about whom you are.

The other thing to remember is that there are a lot of people around us whose actions we cannot control. People talk and behave in a certain manner. And we shouldn't expect our spouse to be able to control theirs either. And every action induces a certain reaction. There will be occasions with flirtatious conversations or actions. We will react to them. Unless we want to be outright curt about not tolerating the actions or words circulating around us, we will react to them in a certain manner. The problem is not that these actions and words are taking place or that we are reacting to them. The problem is when ours or our spouse's mind wants the other to react a certain way and that doesn't happen. Circumstantial reactions are not really given much benefit of doubt.

The bigger problem comes when the jealous spouse puts their feelings to actions. If you are jealous, learn to control your action for the time being, unless your intervention is brutally required. If you feel the pangs of jealousy, remember that your love will go back home with you, when it might be a better time to let them know how you felt. And when you do talk, consider not being accusatory. It's a fact. You were jealous. It's your feeling to manage. You don't expect your spouse to do anything about it, but just want them to know that your feelings of territoriality got touched upon. And you are reminding yourself of the marked territory.

Now consider that sometimes jealousy is induced to evoke a reaction. I know of friends who love to make their spouse jealous, just to make sure that the feelings are still alive. More often than not, it is for people who have become so busy that the expression of love is far and distant. The other spouse uses the jealousy angle to give themselves a little assurance that the love is still alive. It's a good tactic but a dangerous one to evoke at certain times. It might backfire as the other spouse might react in a manner that is no longer under your control. Remember, you always have better control over your reactions than you have over the other person's.

There comes a time in all relationships where you are not sure if your spouse is still as much into it as you are. It could happen in one year from marriage to twenty years timeframe. But it does happen. You are two different people and you are evolving together. As you do so, you also realize that everything you imagined or expected marriage to be might not be all true. For better or for worse, you have to now re-set those expectations. And when you do, you also give the signal to your spouse that you are re-setting. Your spouse might not be in the same spot as you. He/she might have a little lag in that same realization. That's when the gap in expression of love takes place. The other spouse feels that gap. It's non-verbal but it's very much alive between the two of you. When it does happen, most people find it difficult to pick up a can of beer, sit down and talk things out in a light hearted manner.

Imagine a scenario, where you tell your spouse; "Not really how you thought it will be, right? ☺ Difficult isn't it? Do you want to walk back that aisle?" The laughter that follows corroborates that you are still friends and you still have that bond where you can say whatever you have on mind to the other person.

You might be surprised that as easy as the above scenario sounds, it is not that easy to implement for a normal person. Your ego comes in the way. But more than your ego, the fright does. You are scared to know the answer or you are not prepared for what it might be. Your gut tells you one thing but your ears and heart is not ready to accept it and definitely not hear it from your love. It will confirm your fears and then what? That million dollar question is hence left unsaid. Instead, we device ways of trying to corroborate our fears by actions. These actions are to see if the other person still feels the jealousy that will live only when the love still lives on. Evoking or judging the existence of the jealous strands in your spouse helps prove to YOU that he/she still cares for and loves you. After that if there are things that are worrisome about the marriage, you are ready to deal with it. This jealousy evoking tactic probably helps you feel better that all is not lost when you do ask that question.

As smart as we think we are when we pull that trigger of trying to make our spouse jealous, remember you still don't control their actions and reactions. You will pull the trigger, but it might not hit the right target. Are you prepared for that? Imagine that you go into a social event and start flirting with his colleague, hoping he will notice and get upset (or at least show some emotion). Instead, something that we had discussed earlier happens. Your spouse now misjudges this action for need to look around since you are not satisfied with the marital status that you are in. What now? The seed is now embedded.

If now, your spouse was in a position of self-doubt and nebulousness, you have now fed the fire. You have now given a reason to show that it's not just him/her. The thoughts that permeate from there are never ending. Now, you have to do damage control for not your spouse's actions or lack there off but more for your own. Your initial purpose will be marked as a blank because it definitely didn't achieve what it was targeted for. Instead it has now germinated another series of thoughts that can prove to be very damaging.

SOMEBODY... Train me for MARRIAGE!

On the other hand, if your spouse was oblivious to the fact that there was something amiss in the relationship, what reaction would your actions evoke? He/she was just busy at work and had not done a good job of keeping you posted on the things that are on their mind. Instead, their actions have now leads you to feeling as if both of you are not at the same place as you were when you walked down that beautiful aisle. So, you go and pull that trigger. You go out of your way to make your spouse feel jealous to test and see if those feelings are still alive and kicking on the other side. Excellent!

The only problem- now you could start placing those same fears and insecurities that you were mentally blaming your spouse off, into their mind. It's a risk. Don't get me wrong. You could end up evoking thoughts in him/her that re-ignites the passion you felt when you first started dating. On the other hand, what if all you evoke is doubt.

The same thoughts that you were trying to fight against in your mind, could very well be now germinated into that of your spouse. Yikes!

So, long story short, playing the jealousy card is a double edged sword. Be prepared for any kind of reaction.

Personally, if your personality is not such that you are just a little flirty and a little "out there" by nature, don't pull that string to test the feelings of your spouse. Better still, have a drink or two, at a bar, flirt with him/her, and then gently ask if all was OK? Be prepared for the answer in your mind. You don't need to get into the mind of your spouse. Control yours.

The feeling of jealousy is a very strong one. It plays with your mind and your heart. If you don't feel jealous, you might be a little stoic in the expression of your feelings. But also, ask yourself one thing. Do you not feel jealous because your level of feelings has diminished? If so, be honest with yourself. Why is it? It could be that other worldly matters are taking priority in your life. It could be that you are feeling overwhelmed with this new world of married life. It could be that you are no longer in the same spot as you once were with the love of your life. It doesn't need to be that you are looking elsewhere. But it is best to be honest with yourself that you are human (animal) and you are evolving. Hence your emotions might be evolving. This gate-check is more powerful than you think. But once this gate-check is done, what now?

You cannot go back and undo the vows and call it quits. You are committed to this relationship through thick and thin. This is a broader question that we will address in a later chapter which deals with your feelings which have now diminished. But for this one, I will leave you with this one thought. Be honest with yourself. Even if there are situations when you can't be hundred percent honest with your spouse, be honest with your own evolution. That is intrinsically important for your relationship. Dishonest relationships invariably lead to dishonest actions for self-regeneration.

Be yourself first. If you are jealous, say it but try not to act it. If you induce jealousy, accept it and let your spouse know about your nature (if they don't already). If you feel jealousy, control your actions. Speaking out about your feelings might help set things straight versus trying to manipulate them. If you want to induce jealousy, to evoke a set reaction, be careful and prepared that it might not be the exact same reaction that you hoped for. But more than anything else be prepared.

I will leave you with an example of a person I came across once that left me somewhat puzzled. The husband has a very busy work life and extremely odd hours. The wife is a doting mum and a great home-maker. The couple has a house in the country and a condominium in the city. The wife and child spend ninety nine percent of their time in the country home...that's their life. The husband spends seventy percent of his time in the condo to accommodate easy commute to office and odd work hours. A very simple and easy life. The condo is very well decorated. It has two bedrooms, one for their child and the other being the master bedroom. The master bedroom has lovely pictures of their child in different phases of life. The living room has a small picture of the wife in one corner of the room!

It came out later, that the wife had never asked for a picture of hers to be put in the master bedroom. The couple has now owned the condo for five years and not once has she wondered why her photograph doesn't make its way to the bedroom? Is she not ready for the response or has she resigned to the fact that her husband is not the sorts to display her picture. Has she resigned to the fact that her husband doesn't need her picture in the bedroom where he spends seventy percent of his time since he has her in his mind and heart? Or has she resigned to the fact that she doesn't want to know what the answer to any of these thoughts are as long as the marriage keeps running on. Or does she not care? Does he?

I feel strongly that where there is love, there is jealousy. The feelings and emotions don't go away. It's for you to control and manage those feelings. And you can only control your actions, not those of your spouse's.

Being seen as a couple: Now part of your identity

A big struggle for me when I first fully comprehended that I was married was when I would see people viewing me as a couple versus as an individual. Suddenly, I went from being "you" to "you all" or "both of you". Initially there was a certain thrill attached to it. The thrill was exponentially higher when we had started dating but somehow after marriage, the thrill was kind of ... well, frightening! There was strength in number but slowly that started getting to me. As individualistic as I am, I realized that my individuality was diluted. I was now part of a fabric, a partnership versus just being myself. I have to admit, that was a very wrong way of looking at this whole aspect of being a couple. But at twenty six, my reaction was just that, a reaction. There wasn't much thought put into it. And of course, you and I both know that there was no training for me either. Nobody actually came out to me and said, "Girl, your life is now going to be viewed as collaboration, a partnership versus only what you do."

And even if somebody had said that, I don't know how willing I would have been to fully comprehend and understand the impact of those words.

But the truth is now you have entered a partnership. You are no longer standing by yourself. Your decisions are no longer just for you. You are speaking for both of you. You start using the word "We" versus "I" more. You start thinking more in terms of the partnership versus just you. It's natural to let that come across to others but more difficult to fully accept it internally such that you are comfortable with this thought of "We".

But for those who are somewhat afraid to lose themselves to a slightly bigger picture, it is not bad. For those who find it easy to be a part of the crowd without having the fear of getting lost, you have it relatively easier. You know how to keep your sanity without having insane thoughts of what am I losing here? But I wasn't one of them. I was the one who was afraid of losing my individual self to a "We". I didn't want to play second fiddle to anything or anybody. I was my own self.

But here is the funny side of things. Nobody was asking me to lose myself... definitely not my spouse. The idea of this beautiful partnership came around because we were both individuals who found mutual affinity in expressing ourselves and yet enjoyed the power of those forces coming together. Yes, FORCE!

Your individuality is a force. It's a bundle of energy that you are embodying. You focus that energy on things that are material to

119

you. Your spouse is material to you. Your force doesn't get diluted in this partnership that you have embarked on. It only aligns with another one, which will allow it to stay, focused, sharpened and on target... your target.

Enough words on metaphors. Reality.

Your individuality is not in danger. Your marriage is like a partnership. You and your spouse have decided to enter into a partnership of life that will allow you both to flourish and do things together. Remember there is always strength in numbers. You are now both a team. And unless you feel like a team, you will never be seen as a team... as a couple.

I will take you back to the time when you were dating this very special person in your life. How many times did you think "we think alike in many ways" or "I really like the way she/he thinks"? It is either that you found affinity in similarities and found spots where you both were so different that you could learn from each other. That doesn't end just because now you have a common goal of walking the steps of life together. You were attracted to the similarities and the differences. You knew you had things to learn from each other and things to teach. Don't let that initial spark get away from you.

And the way you think of each other is the way the world will see you. They will see you as a couple, as an entity that is a strong partnership between two forces and as a united front. But there are always prying eyes. My only take on this topic is that please is you. Others don't matter. You and your spouse do.

The important thing is that the way you feel towards each other intrinsically is how the world will be able to see you. You respect and honor the person your spouse is. You have an immense amount of trust and faith on your spouse's abilities, dignity and personality. And you also acknowledge your spouse's ambitions and goals in life- they are now a part of your vision for the future, as much as yours are for him/her. If such are your feelings, you don't need to worry about the external world at all. They will get to know. It is not about the hand holding, whispering of loving words or the implicit show of affection that will prove this bond to the outside world. Your natural interaction with your spouse will.

And of course, life that you have now started or going to start is very long. There are bound to be days when you don't see eye to you. People will pry and prod but as long as you remember the absolute real feelings that you have towards each other, they will know not to mess with you. They will always see you for what you are. A team. A very strongly bonded team.

I am sure you realize there are always those around you who seek for slivers of discrepancies, of cracks in the armor such that they can dig deeper. You will always find those around you who have time on their hand and unhappiness surrounding them. These are the people who seek corroboration of their unhappy state of mind and environment by seeking affinity. "Who else is ultimately unhappy but just doesn't know it?" They take it upon themselves to identify you, make you recognize your unhappiness and thereafter bring you into their circle of negativity so that they can feel good about their state of mind and being. Yes, in common terms, we call them the seriously "sad" entities. But as much as we know about them and know not to let them get to us, they somehow manage. That's life and the stupidity of it. These are the people who are seeking chinks in your armor such that they can drill deeper and make the pain hurt more. They are always analyzing you. Always being judgmental about you and what your relationship stands for.

Make sure that they realize that the armor is not breach-able. And the way to show it is not to let them get into your head. That's one place where things just stick. That's a dangerous territory to let any outsider get access to.

But before that you have to be true to yourself. Are you an exhibitionist or not? Do you like the world to know that you are madly in love and it is reciprocated? Or would you rather keep those feelings sheltered and protected from the external world and in a cocoon shared just by the two of you?

If you are more of a private person who likes to keep special feeling somewhat out of the prying eye:

Recall the time you felt the need to enter a party, holding hands and bodily leaning on each other to show how much you loved each other. The honest aspect of that is you both know you love each other. You just want to show what a loving couple you are.

For those who don't care whether you love your spouse or not, it really doesn't matter. It is for those who do care, you are preparing ammunition for a defensive strategy that keeps those very nosy "sad" entities quiet. You don't want to feed them with things to talk about or think about. You definitely don't want to give them the impression that there is anything wrong between the two of you.

On the other hand, if you and your spouse are too busy proving to each other that there are still individuals in the partnership entered, you probably will go out of your way to show that you don't care to show the extra loving side of yourself. Your private life is not for exhibition. You are meant to be seen in that party as an individual. You come as a "we" but there is a definite "I" in there that will be loud and clear in expression, verbal or otherwise. I can bet my meager piggy bank money, that there are always those around you who will react in some way or the other. "Are you guys doing OK? You seemed somewhat aloof from each other as you walked in."

Let me share an example with you. During our first year of marriage, we made friends with this lovely couple. The woman quickly became my good friend and the gentleman was my husband's. At a very early stage of our friendship, it became very evident that their relationship was a little strained. They seemed to have married for the wrong reasons but find it financially and socially difficult to bring it to an end. Also compounding the fact was that there were kids involved. That always makes things exponentially difficult, even if you realize you are in toxic union.

The more we got to know them; we realized that my friend would seek opportunities to put her husband down in front of all of us. In private, she made no bones about her unhappiness. The gentleman took the punches on the chin with a smile and gave back a couple of verbal rounds back once in a while.

But what came across as most odd was the questioning and prying that would take place, publicly and privately. Both husband

and wife would engage us (my husband and I) in conversations privately and otherwise to see how things were between the two of us. Especially during private one on one conversation, the prying would intensify.

And as all couples have, we also had our good and bad days. During the bad days, those prying sessions would be almost parasitic. It felt to me as if she would want to latch on to whatever negativity she could from me and feed on it. She would bring forth her examples/experiences and how these men in our lives behave a certain way. I never found instances where she would actively persuade me to look at my husband's point of view. And my husband felt the same.

If days are good and there was nothing for her to latch on to, she would feed things into my brain. The feeding including behavioral patterns to look out for in my spouse.

Somewhere in our association, both of us realized the negativity we were allowing ourselves to get engulfed in. And also the impact it was having on us. We would be extra exhibitionist of our mutual affection in front of them. Or during those bad marital days, we would seek the social forum (in the company of this couple) to berate each other. They had managed to get into our heads. Big mistake.

The problem was that these were two very unhappy people. As individuals, I am sure they were very capable of being happy and full of positive energy. But somehow the energy turned caustic when it came to them being together. They exuded negativity in each other's company. And negativity seeks companionship. We had allowed them to successfully feed into our relationship for companionship.

But it will be faulty of me to blame this couple for creating the circumstantial negativity (even if it were for small spurts of time). We had allowed them to get into our heads. Human brain is wired a certain way. Certain actions, words and expressions connect our neurons in ways that the data set gets embedded forever. Conditioning.

In the case of association with this couple, we had allowed them to impact our relationship. Our choices at the time were simple. Did we really need to associate ourselves with people who were "sad" entities? Could we have distanced ourselves from them and been who we intrinsically were? Could we have kept the social interaction to the point where they know that they need to be a little careful of what they say to one about the other spouse? Could we have not allowed them to pry into our marital life? Could we have exhibited our united front, our team solidarity through thick or through think, through good or bad days?

Yes, we could have. One can clearly say, well they were able to prey on you, because there must have been something intrinsically weak in the relationship. If the love is strong and powerful, nobody can mess around with it. True but not so much. It is a classic chicken and egg story. Remember, we are after-all humans. We have emotions that go through their ups and downs. And during the downs, we feel weak. A united front also gets challenged.

For those who are wondering, this couple did not cause the divorce. If anything they actually helped us stay away from it for a long time. We, as a couple, had finally gotten our head around the fact that we won't let them get inside our brains and we definitely didn't want to end up like them.

Actions taken: We distanced ourselves from them. During limited social interactions, we made an effort to not encourage questioning and prying. We also didn't encourage topics that will allow them to get into our marital discussions. If and when, they did pull us into those discussions, we brushed them off and spoke of things that were encouraging and loving towards the other spouse.

Result: they backed off. They saw that we were in this together. We won't let them get into our head. And surprisingly, we became more acquaintances than friends with them. The parasitic process was nipped and hence they had to go find others who could feed into their need for corroboration of negativity. We felt free.

Today, being slightly more mature and slightly more experienced, I can wisely say, that was a lot of wasted energy. We could have spared ourselves all the heartache and painful damage to our relationship had we not allowed other to feed into our relationship. All we needed to do was not encourage the first few rounds of discussions whereby our marriage was being brought into question. In reality, the lack of training on marriage had made me inquisitive about their experiences, such that I could be better informed. But that was so unnecessary. I just had to tell myself that my marriage is none of their business. I won't entertain any prying and have no need to know what's happening in theirs. More so, what happens between me and my spouse is definitely not anybody else's business. It is for me and my spouse to germinate, grow and sustain as we deem fit. Our marriage was ours and there is no footprint that I need to seek or adhere to.

The way outsiders see you as a couple, is partly how you see yourselves. If you allow others to interfere between the two of you, somebody will. If you allow others to get into your head about your marriage, somebody will. If you allow others to pass judgment on your relationship with your spouse, somebody will. And I strongly believe, it is nobody's business. Your relationship with your spouse is for just the two of you. If you want to show your love in public, it's because the two of you want to. It is not for others to see it. If you want to stay aloof in a social setting, it is your and your spouse's prerogative. If the two of you are comfortable with the way you get seen as a couple, what others think or care to tell you, really doesn't matter.

What matters are you and your spouse. The individuals who are now a team. The entity that has come together, joining forces to make bigger better things happen.

Friends that you find as couple

Since we were just on the topic of being seen as a couple and the example shared was that of a friend, this might be a good segway into a broader topic about friends whom you are making as a couple.

In one of the chapters, we had discussed being with friends. You and your spouse (most probably) grew up separately and had your own set of friends before you met each other. Then as a couple, you probably got to know each other's friends. Now, as you start your new life together, you will meet more people. The difference this time is you are not making these friends as individuals but as a couple. You are married and that now defines your identity. People will associate connotations to that status. Those associations will lead to direct and indirect mental conditioning of what to expect from these new friendships.

For those who wonder, will I ever need new friends? I have mine and my spouse has theirs. True, but that's a very short sighted view of your life. You are going to evolve in and with your marriage. You are going to grow in your career. You are bound to come across people whom you now meet at work, in your neighborhood, your religious congregation site, and your grocery stores or even at parties. When you meet these people, "let me introduce you to my spouse" will flow out of your lips before you realize it. You want to be seen as a couple. You want to be known as a couple. You are no longer the individual single self who just introduces self.

The interesting thing to note here is that you will soon realize that you and your spouse now start making friends with couples. It is funny what affinity does. But now suddenly, you start seeking companionship with people who are in the same strata of life's journey as you are in. When you were single, you found it easier to hang out with single friends. But now that you are married, you will make friends mostly with couples.

Please know that there is no way you are giving up on your already existing friends who might still be single. Your friendship there is non-destructible. But for new friends, you want those who will understand the frame of mind you are in. With whom you are able to share some of your new experiences.

A friend of mind once said, it is more important for the wives to get along. If the wives make it work between the two of them, the husbands will always find some reason to hang out together. Wise words.

But a few more from me. Remember a few things that will be different in this set of friendship versus the ones that both of you have had thus far.

Your friends from before marriage got to know you as single individuals. They know your personality outside of the marital institution. They recognize you for who you are versus how you look in an entity and a partnership. They know you for your likes, dislikes, hobbies, tastes and preferences. They know your idiosyncrasies and have accepted you for who you are.

The other friends, whom you probably made as a couple, still recognize a single side of you. In their minds, your togetherness was one and one. It wasn't one + one. Subtle but there is a difference. They knew you and your spouse were together but somewhere subconsciously they also recognized that you were two individuals still.

The new friends you are going to make after marriage will only recognize you as one + one = "they". You are no longer you and I. You are now part of a "they". They already see you as an entity. They don't need to recalibrate their thinking to recognize you as a couple.

On the other hand, the fact that they don't recognize you as an individual (till you give it enough time), also suggests that they will

132

take time to get to know you... you as an individual. They will first filter out their understanding of you in a partnership and then try to get to know you as an individual. It will be very rare that you meet and find friends who will click with you as friends just as those from your single days. And even when they do, remember that their point of reference is always going to be the marital entity.

A few instances for you to consider. You will get invited to their homes. They will probably plan the evening with the mindset of what both, you and your spouse, like versus one particular individual. Their point of reference is that you two are one entity and they seek out patterns of your likes and dislikes, tastes and preferences as an entity versus an individual. "They seemed to like white wine." Or "I think they are vegan. That's what she was talking about." These newly found friends (at least in the initial stages) do not see the distinction of the two personalities. If and when this friendship deepens in later years, they may or may not be able to identify you for you. But till then you are part of "they".

For those individuals, who accept diluting their individuality to the bigger cause of "they", are angels. You will ride through this journey like a breeze. You have the DNA to be a part of a crowd and keep your head held high. I can't tell you how much respect I have for somebody like you. And the reason I do, is I struggle to be that person. I am ME. I have never been fond of crowds. And I never learnt how to not be known for what I stand for. Hence, my expectations were a little misplaced.

Somehow I realized why the saying goes that the wives need to get along. The women have far greater expectations from "friendship" than men do. At least most women do. Men, as long as they find one common ground in either sports, politics, drinks or travel, they will have plenty to share without really caring if you are on the Christmas list of the other person or not. Women on the other hand tend to evaluate, analyze, assess and compartmentalize people's reactions. Now you have to realize that I am making broad generalization here. I, myself, have male friends who carry the traits I just described about women with flair and glamor that is enviable. On the other hand, I also know of female friends who couldn't care two hoots as to what the next person does or doesn't do. They are just happily lost in their own being. The generalization is just to raise awareness for you versus framing your thoughts into the belief that all women and men behave in certain manners.

The main issue to keep in mind when entering into couple related newly found friends is to set your expectations. And the other part will be to establish those expectations such that you and your spouse don't create misunderstandings between the two of you. Here is how these two scopes can manifest themselves.

Establishing expectations-

Time; when you meet this new couple, as a couple, you really can't expect them to become your "best friends forever". Time is essential as is with any relationship. But here it is all the more critical that you take baby steps in moving forward because it's not just you and the friend. It is you, your spouse, them and their spouse. It's crowded here!

Getting to know each of them for their individuality; soon you will find that you are making plans to meet up with one of the spouse in the other couple. Either you are going out for shopping sprees with the wife or heading out for a round of golf with the other. Getting to know them is very important. But getting to show them is even more. As with any journey of getting to know each other, you will be inclined to show your personality. But you are new at the personality of partnership. You still carry your individual self and its personality with you. As you rush to make the friendship bonds stronger in an attempt to get to "know them", you will reveal the side of you that is still single. Remember the time we spoke about being seen as a couple? How about you start with the time that you and your spouse got together? Your personality in the entity you are now in is more important than the individual personality you have already inbuilt in it. Your individual personality is bound to be seen through the time that you will give to this new found friendship. Remember, you got together with this couple because you are a couple. Don't try hard to show them the individual in the couple.

Here is why it is important to show the couple personality first. You are fresh with love and fresh in love. That love is what the world needs to see so that at points later on in your life when you do have chinks in that armor from time to time, you have this new fabric of friendship that you are surrounding yourselves in, helps you recalibrate to the points of your life when your eyes were still dreamy with the love and the new life you were entering. Yes, it is a selfish move, but so worth it. Consider it an investment in your future happiness through external influences.

The other reason you need to show your couple personality first is so that you help yourself establish it for yourself. "We love this restaurant on Elm Street that we tried for the first time. Maybe we can all go there together sometime"; works wonders with this new found friendship versus "I love this restaurant on Elm Street. I used to hang out there during my college days. Maybe all of us can go try it out together sometime". Think about the signal or the message each of the messages sends out. One puts you and your spouse on one side with the other couple on the other when you state the couple personality. Your statement still exhibits your personality and preferences, now a part of the entity that you are in. On the other hand when you take your new friend to the "I" time of your life, you are putting yourself on one side and the three of them on the other; the other couple and your spouse. Now you are taking the three of them out to your loved hideout. Now your new friend is busy understanding your personality versus how to relate to your new life in the marital status. A simple statement but heavy with long lasting impact on something or somebody who might be in your environment of influence for a long time to come.

How is this different than the friends that you had from before (before marriage or even before)? Immensely! Your old friends don't need to figure you out. That piece of the process was long done and its water under the bridge. They are now more interested in how the two of you are doing or how you specifically are doing with the new status in life that you have embarked on. They probably know the hangout places from your impressionable days. Again, they know the single personality.

The flip side of this coin is also what you get to know about the other couple. Remember, that "getting to know you" is a two way process. You are also trying to understand what the other couple stands for. Without consciously registering, you are taking in data points of the "we" versus the "I". You are more interested in the "We" but if you hear more of the "I", you will probably be a little cautious. Questions start framing in your mind without you realizing it. Is the bond in the couple strong enough? If so, then why does the "I" speak so loud? If not, where are they in their marital harmony? Some will say, "How does it matter"? It does. Unhappiness in marital status is unhappiness in life.

You don't want to surround yourself with the negative energy that this new found friendship might bring. You seek good positive energy that will energize you from time to time. You don't want your energy to be depleted but to be supplemented.

I hear myself sounding almost selfish. Well, "Almost".

Here is why selfishness in this case is not bad. You are not only helping the two of you (in your marriage) but also the two of them. Imagine trying to get to know two new people at the same time as one, but you are dealing with this negative vibe that keeps coming your way. If you choose to ignore, saying it's none of your business, or trying to be the night in shining armor, you will suffer later. On the other hand, if you give the clear and precise signal that you want to know and associate with happiness around you,

you also help the other side understand that they need to be a little bit introspective.

I will (once again) give a simple example. In our early years establishing our marital couple roots, we sought to make friends with other couples. We came across one whom both my husband and I, spend some energy in getting to know. I got to know her and my husband got to know him. We had our fun days but when it came to truly getting to know each other, it didn't take a rocket scientist to understand that they were just unhappy with each other in their marital status. But instead of doing anything about it, they chose to vent in public and in private. Whenever we met (either one on one or all four of us together), the discussions would invariably harbor along negativities of their marriage. Initially, listening to them and trying to help them out was (for lack of a better word) "fun". We sincerely tried to see how we could help. It was informative to know that marriages could have the dynamics that theirs did. But without the two of us realizing it, it got to us. We started looking for similarities of their marital symptoms in ours. Of course, when we had our little issues, we would blow them out of proportion because we knew how bad it could be. Frankly don't understand how that psychology works, but their negativity had really rubbed off on us. We had become negative in our marriage. Guilty by association.

I don't say that the fault was the other couple's. Absolutely not. They made no mistake (except for not owning up to the truth of their marriage). The mistake was ours. We could not disassociate from them. In our desperation to be with other married couples, we found ourselves in a pool of negativity that ultimately swallowed us as well (blamed to some extent). This was preventable.

Later on in our marriage, when my husband and I, communicated with each other about our true feelings about the other couple, what surprised me was that he also felt that we should probably not have associated with them. "What an idiot I was". I thought I didn't want to deprive him of a new friendship and he thought he didn't want to deprive me. We ended up depriving each other of some happy days that we could have saved. And when we did remove ourselves from the company of the other couple, the freshness that we felt as individuals was also refreshing. Bottom line: stay away from negativity and people with negative energy.

Avoiding misunderstandings when making new friends-

How many times did you have misunderstandings with the friends that you have had for years now? How many times was your then date/friend/fiancé and now spouse jealous of interactions that you have had with others or vice versa? All that is bound to happen again with your new found friends.

The new couples friendship that you are forming is also going to bring forth completely accepting the personalities involved. You might come across a husband who expresses himself very flirtatiously. Or the wife who expresses himself with flair and flaunt. As long as they see you as an entity and you see them as one, you will be fine. You cannot expect your spouse to be able to control their behavior. Just like the topic of dealing with jealousy, do not expect that your spouse is responsible for extracting the reactions from the other person (in this case the member of the other couple). Be a little flexible with your judgements. Give the benefit of doubt to your spouse first and foremost.

A new couple friend that we had formed was just too much fun to hang out with. The only problem was that the husband had a habit that was just pure annoying. He would invariably make a comment or two about my outfits or my hair. Initially, it was endearing because I thought he was just trying to be nice. But slowly realized that more than it being annoying to me, my spouse would feel uncomfortable. But there was nothing for me to do other than dress like a hag every time we met this other couple, to make sure that I did not evoke any such commentary (which personally I couldn't do because of my sense of decorum). I am sure the comments were very innocent and made in good jest but we couldn't go on to find out. Even after making some suggestions on asking the gentleman to not make those comments, he couldn't stop. Think it was more a habit. Ultimately, we gave up. We couldn't carry on being friends with them for long.

You make friends but your spouse doesn't-

A big aspect of this discovery was also that it will be very difficult to sustain friendships where both of you are not equally engaged. If you get along just fine with one member of the other couple, but your spouse cannot finds their company appealing, the friendship is going to be strained and difficult to manage. Make life simple for yourself. Set your priorities correct. The reason you started engaging in this couples friendship was because the two of you wanted to make friends together. If that is not happening, don't push it! What is the point? You will only end up making first your spouse and then yourself miserable. Again, not worth it.

In cases where you get along like a house on fire with your friend in the other couple and your spouse finds it difficult to completely relax with them, turn the tables. There was no rule book that suggested that all four of you have to like each other. Turn the couple's friendship into individual friendship. You can never have too many friends. You can still have the occasional social gatherings where all four of you are engaged but it is more a "nice to have" versus a "need to have". But do your spouse the favor- do not push them towards a friendship that is unnatural. Friendships are the most natural thing that can germinate and grow if they have to. Friends come together and there is a click. If the click doesn't happen, don't force it. You will only end up making others feel miserable.

Do you hear and UNDERSTAND each other?

Maybe I haven't looked at the right places, but would have appreciated a book on communicating with the one you love? My single most difficult topic to deal with in life. You could be making a living making presentations in front of corporate executives, seeking and making decisions worth millions of dollars, mentoring and training others to use communications as an advantage and ammunition, but when it comes to communicating at home with the person who is closest to you, you might be a complete mess. I was.

Communication is probably the most powerful method of connecting with your spouse. You need to be on one page with minimum deviations. Communications don't need to be verbal alone. It can be any form or format as long as it puts you and your love on the same page.

When the two of you were dating, you had an inclination to learn more about each other. You were trying to understand and figure the other person out. You made an attempt to get to know him/her. You made an effort to assimilate your learnings into your life. Once you felt comfortable with your learnings, you decided to lead the rest of your life together. You knew it was going to be a journey where the education about each other will keep evolving. You were willing to take a bet that you will enjoy what you find out. But soon you forget your pure, innocent and well placed intentions. You start thinking that you know your spouse completely. You have him/her figured out. That's where the problem begins. We stop making the effort or attempt to keep ourselves on the discovery process that once so intrigued us. The other problem that arises is that since we are no longer making an effort, we use our old data base to fall back on when it comes to making assumptions. And my dear friend, no matter how much you try to tell yourself, you are way above making assumptions, you will make them. You will make assumptions and presumptuous about your spouse just as they will on you.

Let me frame this as an example. How many times have you heard married couples speak to their friends about their spouse in the following terms; "I don't know what's going on in her mind. I got her a gift which I thought she will like. That's the kind of pendant I had given her when we were dating. But her reaction was strange. I thought she will like it. She used to like them a lot earlier." Think of the words you are using. "She used to".

On a similar count, how many times have you heard something to the tune off..."I can't seem to be able to get through to him about my problems. I don't find the time to discuss things at length with him anymore. Earlier, we would find the time to talk to each other. Now, we hardly talk."

Also know that this metamorphosis of your relationship doesn't need to take years. It could be months after the marriage that these changes are taking place. We just don't pay attention because there are so many other things that are changing in our lives that we are completely engulfed by all the things that are new. We quickly lose focus from all the things that used to be important for us to keep them alive and kicking. We take the connotations of marriage far too seriously. We forget to focus on the true essence of being together.

And this is where communication helps. Let's go back to the time you were dating this special person in your life. What were the means of getting in touch with the other person? Did you call occasionally? Were there fifty texts exchanged during the day? In today's world, was it Instagram, Facebook chats, snapchats or was it meeting up in evenings to have a cup of coffee or dinner together? Hope you didn't let go of those means.

Do you truly know your spouse's upbringing?

I met my husband when he was thirty four years old. He had thirty four years of existence before I could align my energy with his. We would share stories of our childhood, our school and college days and of the fun we had as kids, teenagers, adolescents and now as adults. It was a journey of learning. I was keen to learn about him. He was interested in my life thus far. But we listened, we heard and then we moved on with our life together. Setting up a new life. Somewhere in the process of setting up a new life, we forget to use the learnings of each other's upbringing into perspective. There is profound value in the discovery process of your spouse's upbringing. How did he/she grow up? Was the family rich or poor? What were the family platforms that were made important to them when growing up? How was the house set up? Was it always clean and picturesque or was it cluttered at places, well lived in but very cozy? What did their family put emphasis on? Was it a sports oriented outlook or were they more academically oriented? How did they spend their vacations? What family values did they hold sacrosanct? What family traditions does your spouse speak off fondly?

The list can go on but you get the point. And while you are going through this soul searching process for your spouse, also do the same for yourself. It is important to compare and contrast. There is nothing good or bad about the similarities or lack thereof. It is what it is. But now recognize it. It will help you understand your spouse's reactions so much better. It will help you deal with the new life as you will be able to put a perspective on requests, actions, affinities etc.

Let me start with an example and then elaborate on this topic. My friends met and there were immediate fireworks. They saw, they loved and they married. It was meant to be. I recall the early days of their courtship days. They would hang out all the time. They shared their lives stories. They got to meet each other's families. They were just meant to be together. And they did come together to live their lives together.

The husband came from a family that was pretty much self-made. He had a very close family but one with a rough and economically challenged set up when they were growing up. Their father was academically oriented hence all the kids were inclined to academia versus just otherwise. He had four other siblings and each of them was now very well-off through sheer hard-work and perseverance. And all of them were in academia. But growing up

148

they all lived in a small home, had healthy but conservative food and vacations were a luxury that they indulged in very rarely.

She on the other hand was an only child. Her parents had a comfortable set up for her childhood. They went for comfortable vacations, had a sweet cozy but very well decorated home and she was never in want of anything in life. Her wish was always somebody's command to be fulfilled. She grew up to have a fantastic corporate career and a lovely young lady filled with life and enthusiasm.

The two of them made a perfect pair. Both ambitious. They acted as each other's guides in personal and professional setting. They were usually the talk of social gatherings about their achievements. Couples envied them for all that they had put together. A big house, fancy cars, glamorous clothes, exotic parties and even more exotic personality.

But inside the doors of their marriage, the story was a little different. Only very trusted friends were aware that there was chaos where there seemed peace.

She was often stressed and upset about his lack of discipline in action and thought. She found the home cluttered unless she took special care to put things back together. If things around the home broke, it was months before they were attended to by her spouse.

She found him to be always the last minute worker. Things (if they) got done, would be done at the last minute. The lack of discipline in thought and action drove her up the wall. Even in career, as ambitious as he was, he fell short of the kind of targets she had in mind for the combined marital entity. For him, the work was important. Extending the work with an external network interface was not something he believed in. She knew that his kind of achievement was bound by limits. And how could "they" achieve their goals in life, if you don't put all aspects of your strength into action. She wasn't the kind of wife who would ask for things. She was more than capable of getting them on her own. But she wanted her partner in life to also have the drive that will be at full throttle. How else could they drive at hundred and twenty miles per hour through life?

He, on the other hand, had a laid back attitude when it came to personal life. Professionally, he was well esteemed for his intellectual prowess. Expert at all that he did. But he would rather get the work done and let accolades come his way, versus plan out his next big strategic move to clinch the next promotion. Personally, when he entered the thresholds of his home, he wanted to take it easy. His workspace at home or in office was never structured and organized. But he knew exactly where thing were. He couldn't fathom the intrinsic need to keep things back in their place after use. He wouldn't mind staying with a broken bathroom door for (ever) a long time as long as he didn't have to think about it. He wanted his books to read, his music to listen to and his TV to watch to completely relax. He didn't care how the retirement plans were working, when the next vacation was or what work the house might need for upkeep or enhancement. He was absolutely ok if he stayed in a small little shabby apartment as long as he could have his books and go for long rides. Her insistence on planning for the future, taking vacations in exotic locales, need to buy/wear designer clothes was absolutely beyond him. He had his work clothes and at home, he couldn't care less what he wore. He would get stressed when she would start talking about investments, about the private schools that their potential kids could go to, the need to invite their respective bosses for dinner or the next postal code where their next home should be in. They both loved each other but were having a hard time dealing with the detailed idiosyncrasies. When the right time for the right conversations came, was it a wonder that both of them had eye opening moments? He had not grown up in a meticulous home. It was cluttered all the time. With so many people living under one roof, their home was lived in and anything but presentable. The

151

mindset of the family for the husband was always into academia. Things were not fast paced. It was laid back. Things with intellectual gravitas carried weight for them. He had grown up with the idea that homes without books everywhere indicated it was a home of idiots! As absurd as the notion was, it was his reality and without realizing it, he had that embedded in his DNA. He couldn't care less about the boss, whose intelligence he had very little regard for but would have loved to socially interact more with the colleague who was also writing his own book. His idea of vacations was a hiking trip in the wilderness with occasional stop overs at the Best Westerns of the area. He found better value in spending on a good solid car, a good Bose sound system or a set of first edition books of Leo Tolstoy. Things that either he couldn't afford when he was a kid or things that had intellectual standing.

She, on the other hand, had grown up going to great vacation locales with even better in mind to get to. Her father was a corporate honcho and she knew what it took to climb the corporate ladder. As a kid, they had cleaners coming to their home to take care of the house. Her mum was always particular about the house looking ready for "Home and Garden" photo shoot anytime of the day. Her parents had saved up enough to send her to the best private schools, the best university and provide her all the extra avenues to expand her personality as she could. She didn't have the caliber to go and get a PhD if that was the only profession left on earth for her. But she did know how to manage those who had PhD's.

But with all the intellectual and social bench strength that both of them created being together, they couldn't understand one small thing. Love is what binds them together. And your upbringing is what you carry with you inside no matter how much you try to get rid of it. It is encoded in your system. You have been conditioned to think and behave a certain way by the nature of your upbringing. No matter how much you try, you do reflect some of those conditioned behaviors in your adult life.

Recognizing them and accepting them is the first step. Exhibiting them and either getting acceptance or a work around them is the next.

Here is how the couple put the first and second steps together.

1. Their home had different floors. The husband got the basement floor to do whatever he liked. His books could be thrown around, his papers everywhere, his music scattered, and the wife would not care. She had to mentally train herself not to react to the basement floor (not the husband). If (and those ifs came far and distant), she

walked down to the basement, she would not be judgmental about his space. That was purely his space to do what he wanted. She on the other hand, had the living space on the first floor to decorate and keep as she wanted. If she found anything there that would throw her in a tizzy, she would simply take it and throw it down the stairs. No question asked and none received. Clear demarcation of space. They actually found some humor in this solution. They learned to have fun with this segregation of physical space. Jokes were pulled on each other (but sparingly). But a lot of respect for the other person and their upbringing was created through this process. As for the second floor bedroom areas, he had a basket where he would keep throwing things that he couldn't bring himself to take care off and the basket found its way to the basement till he found the time to take care of them. Books, papers, clothes, everything found its way into that basket and made its way to the basement till he, himself couldn't take it anymore.

2. She, on the other hand, did not continue pulling teeth (his teeth to be precise) about investments and future planning. She was more than capable of doing their retirement

planning by herself. She could make decisions and plan for the future. She gave him intermittent updates on how things were going over dinner and snuggle time in front of the fireplace. But other than that she had the authority (but more-so the responsibility) of taking care of the things that mattered to her more than they did to him. He on the other hand, felt rested and relieved that he didn't have to hear her ask for thoughts, actions and execution of retirement planning strategies. She was more than capable of doing it for the family. He would offer advice to her as and when the ideas or the time came.

3. Vacations were fun to manage. They each took one vacation responsibility each for the year. She planned for an exotic location of her choice while he planned for the rugged experience of his. Each could not ask about the vacation plan from the other. They were surprises. No judgements were passed on the choices. The idea of planning for a vacation moved from "planning for us" to "planning for me". The other person came along for fun and experience. The other person was there for the love.

4. Entertaining was given a lot of independence. Instead of inviting bosses over for meals at home, dinner venues

were selected where all of them could appear and be entertained. This relieved the stress and strain that came with entertaining at home. The husband could tolerate the time invested for social hob nob while the wife achieved her goals. When the right mind set and time came, they would hold open houses. It allowed a lot of guests to come and entertain each other without the added pressure of expectations. Yet it was cozy home setting to allow access to the personal side of their marital entity.

I am sure there were many such solutions provided for them to work things out. They were two strong individuals who came wired a certain way before they were united. The wiring mechanism was a product of how and where they were at different stages of their lives. Learning to recognize, accept and assimilate them into your life will lead to reduction of stress and misunderstandings now and later in life.

Who the Dominant in your relationship? Identify it

This topic is a little difficult to write about now in light of the renewed enlightenment people have about the word "Dom" and "Sub" since the huge success of "Fifty Shades of Grey"! No I don't intend to put sexual connotations to this topic. That's for later! This topic is to recognize who is the stronger personality in your relationship. And somehow I can immediately read your reaction to the realm of stronger personality. Let me first start by saying – there is absolutely nothing wrong with being the beta in your personal life. It makes you even more powerful in life in general. Let's elaborate.

If you take a minute to think about the first few things that come to mind when you say the word "strength". You will realize that the first few things are always very masculine. You are conditioned to associate the word strength with men and what they stand for. And there is absolutely nothing wrong with it. Men, by nature of birth and evolution, are encoded to have strength. They are the hunters, providers, defenders and the protectors. Why should women feel bad about this aspect of natural evolution of thought and expectations?

Instead women embody the strength of a man. That's even more powerful in some cases.

But keeping the sexism side of strength aside for some time, each gender brings different strengths to the table when they come together. Remember the time when you walked back after a date with a very special person, thinking "wow! We are alike in so many ways yet not so in many others". That aspect of dissimilarities along with having congruence with your partner is what drew you closer. You are not meant to be the same. But what each of you get to the table is equally important.

But one of you has a slightly stronger personality than the other. And when I say that, you usually think of the man. You will be amazed how women can wield their power without you fully comprehending it. My mother is a prime example. Before I start on her, let me first say that I love her immensely. She is a wonderful inspiration in my life. And an extremely strong woman.

A very soft spoken lady with very limited education, she is a quintessential home maker. Dad was the macho "man of the house" who "wore the pants". But mom's influence is amazing. She and my dad have this marital ritual. Every night and early morning, they would talk. They talked about everything. They exchanged each other's day stories, thoughts, ideas, opinions and pick on each other's brains for path forward on special topics. The special thing about these talks was that they would happen in the realm of their bedroom. Nobody else was allowed in there. It took me a better part of my adult life to fully understand what the full significance of those one-on-one conversations used to be. My mother has this fantastic way of picking a topic of strategic important to the family, delve into my dad's brains for his thoughts and somehow manage to re-direct them into how she wants things done. My poor dad would come out thinking that those were always his ideas that my mom had corroborated. My very masculine and strong dad had no idea that he was merely the messenger most of the times. He would implement decisions made for the house that were originally my mom's ideas. I am sure he agreed with most of them, or else he would have found it difficult to go through with them. But on the ones that he didn't agree, he had to face silent resistance (never loud or spoken but always subtle) that was more a nuisance to deal with than if there had been an argument. And after years of marriage, my dad knew that if he had to do what he wanted to do outside the home, he didn't need these silent treatments. They stressed him out. Hence, he would much rather fall in line with what my mom had wanted him to implement versus go against the "very loud" silence that would otherwise come his way. And they have now been married for thirty five happy years.

Here was the secret. They each knew their strengths in the areas of their interests. Mom couldn't care less what Dad did at work. He could be moving earth for all she cared. But when it came to her world, her humble little home and family that she put all her energy in, she cared. A lot! And that's where she (in all honesty) knew more about than dad. But of course, Dad's ego wouldn't allow her to call all the shots, so she made him call the shots. But they were her shots.

One phrase that I had always heard was "who wears the pants in the house". A very valid but very sexist question. These days either of you could be wearing the pants. Just wear them with flair. That flair will only be exhibited when you truly know and recognize your true strengths.

A small mental exercise for you.

Passion- Go back to your list you made of things that make you happy. Which of those items on that list makes you feel, "even if I don't get it from my spouse, I want to get it myself"? Those are the items that you are truly passionate about. You want to strive for those aspects with or without help.

Capabilities- Who are you? Do you know yourself? Are you good with numbers, people, décor or kitchen? Once you get to that capability list, turn that around and ask, do you want to really use those abilities?

For example- I am actually a decent cook. I can put a meal together in no time and one that is not just a run off the mill meat and potato meal but one that has people lingering on the dinner table. I do have that ability but I do not like spending time in the kitchen. I know I can do it and am good at it. But I would rather spend time on getting the home ready for the dinner; have an exotic presentation for the meal versus preparing it. Hence, my ability to cook does not match up to my desire to cook.

Now, do you know your list of capabilities (ability matched up to desire)? This is where you are comfortable? This list is what signifies what comes from within versus things you can do.

Now combining the list of passion and capability is where your heart lies (metaphorically of course! Your heart is with your love in reality). And this is where you will wear the pants no matter how much you try.

Citing another example of my friend's household. He was an operational excellence genius. He could make the world a better place a second at a time. She was a home maker. She could make a house look like a picture from a magazine. And she loved to entertain. When it came to people coming at home, she was the one to pull all the shots. When it came to what happened with the kids, she pulled the shots. When it came to where to go for vacations, she pulled the shots. He neither objected not interfered with anything around the home. She wore the pants in the house! No two words about it. He was proud of this fact. He always said "Thank God I am good in office and she is good at home. I am the boss in office but she is the boss at home." It is easy to say those words but very difficult to implement. He was a genius (just like my mom). He wanted her to wear the pants in the house such that when he got back from being the boss in office and wearing the pants all day, he will be taken care off. He wore the pants outside. His job was to earn the money to secure their present and future. Where he invested the money, how he invested, and what insurance to buy was his problem. She didn't know and didn't want to know. She conveyed to him what she needed to keep running the home front to her desire. He would either say "yes, we can do that" or "give me a little bit more time, we are not there yet to take up that expense". They worked together as a team. The kids knew the mom would make all decisions when it came to their lives. They knew dad was an outside person. And they lived happily ever after.

Now, a different scenario. Another set of friends. Wife is a successful professional and result oriented. Husband a successful academic, who valued the ventures of time and mental harmony for him to produce the work of art research that his life was devoted to. Both successful but both very different personalities. She cared for future investments, retirement planning and advancing their socio-economic status. He cared for the peace that allowed him to enjoy life, spend time with the kids/family and devote his strength to pursuit of intellectual advancement. When it came to kid's studies, homework or picking out which extracurricular activities for the children will strengthen their future, he wore the pants. When it came to making sure their combined hard earned money was bearing fruits, she wore the pants. And each of them was completely comfortable with their roles. The kids knew whom to turn to for decisions in their lives. The family knew who to turn to when it came to which zip code will the family live in five years' time. And they lived happily ever after.

So, now that you have defined who the dominant and sub is in different pieces of your life, you should define, accept and assimilate this aspect between the two of you. Let me take one more second to emphasize the statement "the two of you". This is your relationship. Nothing and nobody else needs to come in between. And you have to make a conscious effort to block external influences out. And external influences are bound to make some sunny days cloudy for you.

Do you think it was easy for the couple who had the wife being the dominant in the home and the husband as the sub? They had friends and family whisper negativity in their ears. "Don't you think your husband should take more responsibility in making some decisions regarding schools? After all, it is a combined responsibility. How can you let him wash his hands off this duty?" or better still "How can you let your wife decide what investment management company your retirement funds should be allocated with? Shouldn't she be taking care of the kid's homework and you making the decision on the investment front"?

People around you, especially those whom you allow to get somewhat close to you, think it is their god given right to pass on their judgments and opinions to you. People inherently are very interfering species. They like to meddle in each other's business. You can't really disown them for being who they are naturally supposed to be. It is your duty to keep your thoughts strong and strengthened.

For a husband to be proudly stating; "I don't have a clue and don't give two hoots to what happens on our investment front. She is good at it and she does it. If you want to know anything about those, ask her. I have no interest in that topic", it takes courage and strength. You have now come out and stood behind your wife and told the rest of the world, "don't you dare". For a wife to be proudly confessing "He is better with the kids and their work. I am the mom but he is just a great dad. He knows the kids inside out and knows what's good for them. If he makes a decision about them, I know it will be the right one"; takes an equal amount of courage. For a woman, it is naturally expected to be the home maker, kid's caretaker and the peace maker. Instead if she allows the better of the two of them to take that dominant position and be proud of herself in her skin, kudos to her. She is also sending a strong message to the world that doesn't mess with my mind or with that of my husband's.

Now the two of you are a team!

Again, this relationship you entered in is for the two of you and for the love it embodies. It has nothing to do with the rest of the world. The world will speak. It is for you to block the noise out and concentrate on all that is truly important.

That's where both of you are dominantly strong together.

Interference from outsiders: Always!

As we were just discussing in the previous topic, this is bound to happen. We are surrounded by influences, with people. People, by sheer biological nature, find it very easy to start thinking about other people. But unfortunately, the process doesn't stop to thinking. It will morph into comments, glances, questions and judgments. And because we were designed to listen, we listen. And because we are designed to listen, we absorb these external influences in our subconscious level and think about them ourselves.

When I got my first car, I was thrilled. I was ecstatic. My first car bought with my own money. I took a friend of mine out for a drive. She loved it too. But before getting off, she asked, "Does it not have heated seats? The next car you buy, get the rear and front view cameras and the heated seats". I smiled and told her I loved the car "just the way it was". While driving back home, I kept telling myself "this is all I can afford right now and it's the best car in the world". But soon thereafter I noticed something about me. While showing off my new priced possession to my other friends and family, I would speak of all the great features that had me sold on buying this car. But I would also add "So, this doesn't have the front and review view mirrors and the heated seats. But I liked it still. Love the way it drives and how smooth it feels on the road."

Hold on! Nobody else was commenting on this car not having the two features missing. Why was I pointing it out to them? That's because it was playing in my head. My friend's words had entered my head and were echoing there. My proud buy was now lacking a few features instead of all the stuff that it had! All of a sudden, I was thinking about what it didn't have, versus what it does and how proud I am of having bought a car with my own hard earned money.

Such is human nature. The example of the car was to get you to think about the context of influences. We get influenced no matter how much we try not to. It takes a very strong person to state and follow through that they will not let others influence them. Now, let's take it back to the marriage which either you are about to enter or have entered.

You fell in love and you want to spend the rest of your life together. Be true to yourself and ask. Did you seek affirmation or confirmation from others around you before you did that? Hopefully it was a decision that came from only your heart, but you probably told a few friends or close family members around you to see what they think? This is very natural. You probably did this such that you can see it in their eyes, what they truly thought of this big move in your life. Nothing wrong with it. Even if they showed disapproval, you didn't care. You were in love and you were going to move on with the decision of your heart no matter what. But our tendency to seek the corroboration and approval from other influencing factors around us doesn't end. We might stick to our guns and continue to do what we truly want to do, but somewhere in our consciousness, we have now a new set of data that says "Alex did not really think it was a good idea. I wonder why? What did she think that was wrong with the two of us spending the rest of our lives together?"

Similar judgments are made by people around you even after you are married. You will be making decisions of where and how to stay, what to do, where to do and whom to associate with. This environment that you are creating for your new life is going to be influencing some of your future decision, whether you like it or not. You will be looking around to seek corroboration and approval from external influences. You might still go ahead and do what the two of you want to do, but somewhere in your brain (which is almost like a computer chip by itself), the data will get stored about how your environment reacted to your decision/choice.

Be careful. That's the first thing I will start with.

Surround yourself with people who understand you and are non-judgmental. Difficult as it is to find people who have the same desires and wishes, personalities and preferences as you do. But try. Surround yourselves with people who at least think like you. I know this is against conventional thinking. In life, we are told that surround yourselves with people who are different than you such that you are able to see all sides and dimensions. True! But in marital life, surround yourselves with people whom you have a natural affinity with. Not just those you like to spend time with just because they are different.

The difficult aspect of this advice is how do you get to choose your relatives? You don't! But the good side of this quagmire is that you know them and hopefully know how to ignore their words when you realize that all you are getting is venom and nothing substantial or helpful. During the engagement party, my friend was introducing her new fiancé to all her extended family. Some of them were people whom she hadn't met in a long time. There were others whom she considered close and important. One such "close" and "important" person leaned over towards her, smiled and whispered "I always thought you will marry someone slightly better looking and slightly richer, like the other Russian guy you were dating". I am sure you realized that "relative" quickly relegated herself to a slightly demoted position in influence sector for my friend. But the damage was still done. In bad days of her marriage, the question did pop in my friends mind if she had said "Yes" a bit too soon. What if she had waited for her slightly richer and slightly better looking possibility! In reality, she never viewed her then Russian boyfriend as better looking or rich when she was dating him but suddenly she was viewing her husband from the lenses of her relative's eye and making comparisons that otherwise didn't originate in her mind.

Something similar happened to me as well. And I can safely say it did leave an impact. After my wedding, during a normal family gathering, one of my husband's beloved cousins (who neither approved of me nor did she like the gift that I had bought for her home) made a snide little comment about how wonderful the vase was that my now husband's ex-girlfriend had bought for her from Rome. Her words had left a small scar in my heart about how significant this ex-girlfriend must have been in my husband's life to have been so close to his extended family. Fertile is the mind of a normal mortal! And rest assured this was a conversation topic that my poor husband had to explain himself out of for many days to come. Unfortunately, his cousin went scot free but he and I spend a few days agonizing over absolutely nothing.

It will be easy for me to say don't listen to others. Unfortunately, the human body design doesn't allow the much needed switch off button for our ears. We can manually shut out nose and not breathe. We can shut our eyes and not see; we can shut out mouth and not eat. But how do we shut our ears and not hear. Even with the greatest attempts, the most unfortunate things are spelled out when we are least expecting. Hence the time to plug your ears with your much needed ear phones is always a "bit too late". So we just need to learn and train our brains on how to process the information received.

The solution actually for this is very simple. What is truly important? Is it important that there was a life for your spouse before he met you? Is it important that your spouse is "slightly less good- looking" than your previous one? You decided to make a life with this person next to you. That's what's important. Training your mind to stay focused on the simple beauty of your decision, passion, feeling and emotion is all that is important. People will speak and they have every right to. Similarly, you have a right to smile and ignore. You are also well within your right to either put this external influencer in their place (rudely or otherwise) so that they know not to mess with you or your mind. You are also well within your rights to mentally or verbally tell yourself "this doesn't matter" or "is it really worth having heart ache over" or "where is the value in giving my thoughts and energy to such useless words". Jolting yourself with these questions helps the mind from deviating to paths that are neither productive nor useful for your psyche or that of your spouse's.

Ultimately, what matters is that the two of you have chosen each other to spend the rest of your lives. You come home to each other. You will grow old together. You will make a life together. The rest of the world is just your stage. The rest of their words are just background noise.

Being Transparent

Are you truly ready to be completely transparent with your love? Somehow I recall, having a mindset and being mentally conditioned that once you are married, you should always tell your partner everything about your past and your current life. Today, again, a little bit older and a little bit wiser, I would say let's rephrase that statement.

Tell your spouse everything from the point of when you are in the marital status together. I know it goes against conventional thinking but be careful about what you relay from the days when you were single. It's a judgment call.

A couple I know off has this amazing set up. The husband was a trader by profession in his very formative years. And a successful one at that. He enjoyed life to the best of his ability. And when I say enjoy, I mean it in every sense of the word. Think trader and now add enjoy. Yes. Everything that comes to mind and everything that you read about or watch in the movies was his life. Single, very successful, in London, surrounded by pretty women and even prettier hang out places, he did what all testosterone boiling male would do. He thoroughly enjoyed life. Safe and sensible but enjoy he did. And then at the age of twenty eight, he decided to tie the knot with this very sensible lady, five years older than him and one who bought sense and sensibility to different strata for his life. He settled down. He turned his energy into his married life. Worked hard and built this very good life for the family. A house in the city, a sprawling house in the country and one on the beach for vacations. He had invested sensibly and reaped the benefits of it even more so. Had grown through the ranks to have left the world of traders but now only managed them. A book worthy life.

After twenty years of being married, if you ask him what his wife thought of him. "Sensible, very serious business man, excellent provider and a great dad". And now ask him if his wife knows of the life he led before he got married? No. She has no clue. Yes, he did share that he did date other people and has no other illegitimate children but other than that, no further details were shared. She in turn had shared that she had dated other men and lived life as any beautiful woman with a strong personality would live but nothing more and nothing less. Again, all safe and nothing to worry about.

When I first heard about this relationship, I was (once again) stumped. How does this happen? How can a husband and wife not share intimate details about each other's past adult life with the other? Yes, they knew of each other's upbringing and lifestyles but not the details of how colorful or colorless their lives were when they were in the dating scene. And funnily enough, neither of them wanted to know. Today, again, a little bit older and a little bit wiser I have to ask; "Isn't that kind of smart though?"

Every couple has a ground zero. When you came together, you had this instant connection and you felt drawn towards each other. You also went on an exploratory tour of each other's lives. But is it important to share the details of who all were in it that could have potentially taken your spot in the other person's life? Isn't that information that you say is not important right now but data that gets stored in your brain. And the brain is a powerful machine. It will pull out this data when the right time and inopportune moment comes. A fight, an argument or an impulsive need to state a point, and boom! Out comes that memory disk that had stored that you had behaved in a certain way with a certain person in your single life. And out comes the pattern recognition theorem, the congruency model of your past with your present and so on. Suddenly one of you has your words thrown back at you. Suddenly you have demons from your past standing in the room with you, uninvited by you at least. And yes, many a time's those demons and their stories did not get registered in your spouse's brain as it exactly was but more how they can paint the picture from their point of reference.

Don't let this happen to you. Be a bit more cautious. No, I am not asking you to hide things from your spouse. What I ask is for you to be smart. More than harming yourself, you are probably harming your love more. You are injecting thoughts and visions into the other person's brain that is going to sit there in some form or fashion. The fact that your spouse can and will pull things out from the memory banks also suggests that you put it there. It isn't fair to the other person.

Again, ground zero. You have started a life with a special person. This is the life you have chosen. You had to have the experiences you did to make you understand who you truly are and what you truly want. You had to live that past to value the life you are about to enter.

Just like the life of the trader. He had to go through the different aspects of life that defined him as a trader, as a business man, as a provider. But once he tied the knot, he wasn't doing it with one of those women who just fell for the money or the fame. He stood next to a woman who was grounded and who valued him for who he was today. Not what he was. His life before his marriage was important for him to value the journey he was embarking on with this precious woman...his partner for the rest of his life. And they live happily.

But all this is also dependent on the kind of person your spouse truly is. And that's a discovery you have to do for yourself. So don't rush. It is a marathon not a sprint.

Go slow and go steady. Understand what makes your spouse happy and secure. If he/she wants to know, state things to the level they are able to assimilate without hurting them. Don't judge them from the standards you have for yourself. They are not you. You might be completely comfortable with knowing that your spouse had a very colorful life before they met you. That the single personality was all about exploratory. He/she wanted to find themselves and what they liked. And you might be completely comfortable with the thought that after all that exploration, he/she chose you to spend the rest of their life with. That should say something.

But just because you are able and willing to take that for the profound value that you have put on this union, doesn't mean that your spouse will be able to. So don't put your past on the table. And don't burden them with things that are pretty weightless for you.

Understanding your spouse's mindset about values in life and then moving forward is the first step. The second will be dictated by how much your spouse has an appetite for.

Mind you, curiosity is something that we all carry in our DNA. That's the reason we were able to evolve. But this curiosity is a double edged sword. Be careful with how much you want to play with it. You open that door of reveling and the next thing you know, the questions start pouring. The more you reveal, the more they come. So you have to decide when you want to close the door now, especially if you have had a past that was Picasso's work of art!

But if your mindset is to not care about the past, you are a truly special person. You and your spouse might be completely comfortable not wanting to share or know what happened in each other's sexual lives before the two of you got together. But what about the external influencers again? Remember, they are all around you.

Not those others have an ulterior motive of creating conflict and rift between the two of you. But be prepared for the occasional slip of a joke, share of an incident of good old days from an old friend or family member, where a ghost from the past comes back into the room (uninvited by the two of you). And that is when the strength of your bond gets tested again.

It takes a very brave woman and even braver man to stay strong at those times and not let those words affect you. Suddenly you feel crowded. And that is a good time to remind you of "ground zero". You and your spouse have started a new adventure and embarked on a partnership of life. Your life started when the two of you came together. What happened before was not your business. And that is the thought that you should remind yourself off. That thought is the greatest show of solidarity you can exhibit to your spouse. The fact that you won't allow others and other influencing factors to come in between you and your love, exhibits the strength of mind, body and heart that you spoke about when you took your vows. Your ground zero defines the start of something special. Remind yourself of the special feeling you have for the person who stood beside you. This person had to live that previous life to come towards you. It had to happen. And you should be thankful for that past to have happened. But now the two of you are together. The two of you chose each other and not those ghosts to lead life's journey through.

By not letting these external influences affect your solidarity, you show a renewed level of respect and love for each other.

And NOW... you have your team!

Learn to LET GO

If you take away nothing from this book but this, my efforts will be worth it. This aspect of married life has to be something that can really make or break it. And yes, this is coming from the same person who has been humming in your ears about how the sustenance of your individual self is extremely important for the marital life. But learning to let go is equally important. The first is relatively easier since your individuality is something that you choose to subdue from time to time for various circumstances. But letting go is not something that is encoded in you. You have to make a conscious effort in telling yourself to do so. You are designed to let go. You are designed to hold on to things, close to heart and mind. But letting go allows you to grow more in the marriage as an individual and as a team member.

Have you ever wondered how your parents survived the multiple years of marital bliss? Do me a favor and ask them if it was all true bliss all the time or was it always a work in progress. I think we both know the answer to that question. "Bliss" in the context of marriage is a highly over rated word. But we usually don't know that when we are in the epiphany of courtship "bliss" and dreaming about the prospects of a "happily ever after". And there is a "happily ever after". Please don't let me shatter your hopes for that. But it is more in a broader scope of the word marriage versus on a microscopic scale for life. Days can be rough. Learn to let go. The expectation that each day of marital journey is going to be like that exciting date that actually convinced you that this person next to you is IT.

As many of you are smirking at the above said thinking, "we know that", let me elaborate some more. When I say days can be tough, you have no idea how bad it can get some times. It gets tougher because our expectations (whatever they are) come crashing down. Our hopes are not met. Our wishes are not always fulfilled. And we get disappointed. And human nature dictates that when we are disappointed or upset, we react!

This reaction is something that we can and need to work on. Remember, your spouse is still a separate person. As much as you love each other, think alike and have aligned hopes/dreams, the other person is going to work differently than you do. You cannot control their actions and reactions but can temper down yours. You are in control of yourself and nobody else. But most of us forget that. We want to control it all. But the most important mistake that we make is that we think we are in control of ourselves. We lose control of ourselves all the time. When the network in us fires up, there is no telling what might come out.

Let me start with a small example and build it up to where things can have a long term impact.

My friends when they got married had already lived together for six months before that. You would think they would kind of know each other pretty well by then. Unfortunately for the wife, the expectations changed some since the single but living together days. Without sounding crass, she now knew for sure that she will be taken care off. Her now husband is a successful investment banker who, needless to say, can afford to take care of her. But the investment banker had to work his way towards success through a rather struggled childhood, student loans and disciplined lifestyle. He could not afford to take care of a lot of things but knew the value of being able to. He could afford to throw a thousand dollars on a lamp without a clinch but would rather look for something similar and yet economical within reason. I, personally, have a lot of respect for such a personality. And so did his now beautiful wife.

After marriage, the wife started upscaling the brands of many of their household items. Suddenly, instead of buying at Trader Joes, grocery came from Eataly or Whole Foods. Instead of buying a regular washing detergent, she would opt for the most expensive Tide that there was to have.

But nothing had materially changed in their economic status from the time they were living together versus now that they were married. Only the perception had changed. The risk factors of dating had diminished.

At one point, when the husband enquired on why the monthly expenses had almost tripped, his wife took it to heart that he didn't trust her with her judgments. That he wanted to micromanage the household decisions and restrict her independence and freedom. You can imagine the next stage of this conversation. Husband wants to explain but questions. Wife explains but more emotionally than factually. Things get outside the boundaries of household purchases into "is this how things are going to be?" To "you cannot dictate what I do and don't do. You don't trust me enough to make a simple decision of grocery purchases." Reactions and actions went into a whirlwind! Groceries, detergents and delicacies were all forgotten. Now it was about the emotional connotations associated with an American Express monthly statement.

Imagine a different reaction to this situation. The husband states he has concerns about the monthly expenses and why that is important to him. Explains a little bit about his mindset of being frugal at places where they can afford to be to build a more stable future together. Wife explains that she thought she will try out different brands to bring somethings different in their lives. A small token of a new life with some new lifestyle choices. But both agree that a more stable future is worth so much more than a sustained new lifestyle. They both focus on things that are truly important and yet find a path whereby both can do what they want to do within reason and with respect for the other person's wishes. Remember, she was not buying those things for charity. They were for the household she is building. He wasn't being unreasonable on being frugal. He is working towards a future for BOTH of them. The focus on "them" was more important here. And they can find a way out of this small but messy situation.

So, many of you are sitting back and thinking; "this is so petty. This will not happen to me." You, my dear friend, are in for a surprise. It might not be the groceries and it might not be the American express statement. But you will have your share of these small, insignificant situations that get blown out of proportion and where both parties forget to let go.

Letting go doesn't mean that you have to forget about things that you truly want to do. Letting go means, focusing on one important factor... your love. You didn't decide to get married to buy groceries from a fantastically exotic location. You decided this person is the partner you want to spend the rest of your life with because of your love. Focus on that.

Where you find yourself losing control of a situation and yourself in it, because a certain emotional cord is strung, ask yourself this one question; "IS IT WORTH IT?" That should clear your head immediately.

Is it worth having this nasty day and these even nastier words pierce through your heart and mind for the sake of detergent? Is it worth it to have those very hurtful words hang around in the air for many days to come and take away precious time from your togetherness for the sake of a $300 increase in your monthly expenses? Yes, sometimes that $300 dollars per month can go a long way for the future, but you get the point.

While I write about "learning to let go", I am also fully aware that it is easier for the smaller and more insignificant things and more difficult for those that might really matter to you.

Remember that when two people come together, there is bound to be friction from time to time. Accepting that (and sometimes saying it aloud such that your ears can hear those words) might help you walk through these difficult situations where you might find it difficult to "let go".

Let's take a slightly more difficult situation to wrap our heads around the pickle that this can create.

A couple I knew off once shared this very personal story off their lives with me, that I think might give you a glimpse of how emotionally straining life can be, where "letting go" can be rather difficult.

The husband hailed from a family of five siblings (all brothers) with him being the youngest. The wife was from a smaller family of three siblings where she was the oldest. The personalities were of course text book. When the time for their first born came around, his family started bringing in all heirloom baby furniture that have been in the family for years. All children of the husband's side of the family had used a particular crib, a stroller, a swing and so on. She, on the other hand, wanted the latest designs for her first born. She wanted to decorate her child's room with the furniture that she and her husband would go and hand pick. She wanted to create dreams for that child in that room. After persuasion from both sides of the equation, the heirloom furniture started pouring in. She would come back one day and find that the crib had been set up and the men of her new extended family were gloating about all the stories that each of them had to share. Next she heard that she was already the proud owner of a beautiful but age defining perambulator which had been used by the oldest child (who was now ready to go to college) of the oldest brother!

Even though her husband knew what she wanted for the first pregnancy for both of them, he could not bring himself to say no to the furniture that all children of his family have used. More-so, there was a part of him that wanted his first child to also use the same furniture. It had an emotional significance for him as well.

This topic was a cause of a lot of emotional tug-of-war for the two of them. She felt betrayed to some extent. He felt she had no value for his family traditions. She felt her wishes were not a priority for him. He felt he was expected to cow down to all her wishes at the cost of his own. Egos kicked in. Fancy words were once in a while exchanged. Those words didn't keep their boundaries just to the topic of the furniture and room setting for the imminent new life but extended it to many other hidden feelings and emotions which helped corroborate each of their cases.

Please ask yourself this one question. "What the hell was truly important?"

Was the crib or the stroller really the topic or was it everything that they couldn't put their fingers on that came into the picture? Pregnancies are known to have their own emotional roller coaster rides. Added to that, there was the pressure of external influencers and expectations that this couple had to deal with. Both of them were trying to do something similar; create memories for themselves and their first born. The one that this new born will enter into and be known as and for. What the couple did was making some bitter memories for both of them about the room and its contents. The tension created was just not worth it but somehow they had lost control of their reactions. Somehow they had lost focus on what was truly important.

The existence of the silent and not so silent influences in their situation was not helping the couple. The influencers did not realize that they had a part to play in this drama. The brothers banter about the furniture and the stories their deceased parents had shared with them about their childhood. The wife's friends sharing the names of the latest brands of user friendly and adorable furniture available in the market and being purchased by the celebrities.

The humorous side of all this was that the child for whom all this was being set up for really wouldn't care two hoots about the furniture. They wouldn't know the difference between the antique versus the latest. They wouldn't care as long as they had smiles filled in that room. They would only go for the security and the happiness that comes with being an innocent child. But instead two mature adults had decided to make it about themselves.

When one sits with this above stated situation, one wonders, whom would you ask to let go? Would you ask the husband to let go of his family traditions or the wife of her hopes? A difficult situation. But in the same breath, one also wonders had they taken the time to sit and express to each other the true significance of the furniture? Had they asked themselves one thing "Is it worth it?" Is it worth having all this heart ache and drama, the bitter memories created at a time when you are supposed to come even closer together? Absolutely not. You don't need to be a rocket scientist to know that. But emotions get the better of us and our reactions get out of hand before rational thoughts can kick in. That's what makes us human and we better appreciate it.

Imagine the situation discussed above but now where each of them learns to let go. They can each have a few pieces that are from the heirloom while some that are latest? If money is not the issue, use the heirloom furniture in one room and the latest in another? God knows, you don't keep the child in one room only? They could also just simply sit back and ask the other person on how to deal with their own personal emotional strain. Just simply stating that you really don't want to argue but want help in seeking a solution brings down the walls of war immediately. You and I both know that.

How about being honest? Would you rather have the fancy furniture (old or new) or have smiles on each other's faces when you plunge into the next phase of your lives. Would you rather fill your home with the joys of sweet memories versus creating a rift when you need to come together the most? But don't deny the fact that these things are important to you. Stating it for the other person that it is important to you, helps the mind of the other person think of a mutually conducive solution versus running towards their own wants and wishes. They immediately become amicable to finding a solution that works for both of you versus one.

When you learn to let go of your emotional baggage and more importantly your ego, the other person has nothing to work with against you. Have you ever considered that? You live with this person. He/she knows best on how to get under your skin. And when the mood is not right to play with it, they will get under it.

They know they can. They do it without realizing it but they do. And you allow them to because you haven't mastered the art of "letting go".

Now, be careful there. If you let go of things that are truly important to you as a person, without the other person realizing that it is important to you, you are bound to do yourself an injustice. The other person is not a mind reader. Your spouse loves you but is not God Almighty. He/she is not supposed to read your mind for your wants and true wishes. You have to verbalize it for them. Or at least express to them in some fashion.

The risk of not expressing is that your spouse might think that your wants were really not that important in the first place or else you wouldn't give up fighting for it. And they are right. People usually don't give up fighting for things that they truly deeply want.

Expression without confrontation is the key. You learn to let go with the right level of expression. That's where communication becomes essential.

For the soon to be parents couple, a simple conversation and asking your partner about how to overcome the emotional obstacle you were facing with letting go of your want (even though you respect and want to fulfil the other person's wishes), would have helped. The other spouse would have fully comprehended the true significance of their furniture wishes.

Well, to finish the story for this particular couple, they didn't have this conversation. One of them did let go. The wife. She let go of her want for her first born to have the latest and the best for the sake of the husband's wants of heirloom continuation. She resented the furniture that came in. Her resentment extended to her brother-in-laws because "they were the ones who influenced her husband." Years later, a little bit wiser and a little bit older, when she relates this story with the same emotional venom, her husband realizes how her dreams had been shattered. All he says; "why didn't you tell me that it meant so much to you?" He also realized that being the youngest, he was so used to having things handed down to him, that he forgot that it really wasn't that important. "It wasn't worth it." But the damage was done. They are not going to have the first born journey to walk through again. Some words could have saved that!

We, as humans, mastered the art of communication and evolved to a different level when we learned how to speak. But we are still evolving on how to use the words right. 'Miles to go before we sleep!'

But if two phrases can help you make journeys for you a little easier, try the following-

4. "Is it worth it?"

5. "I need to let go. But I need to let you know what I am letting go off."

Pause to think about the message that you are sending to your love. That they are more important than other things you held important thus far. That is truly powerful for the life ahead. By learning to let go, you learn to be much closer to the person who truly matters. And they in turn learn the value of love in the life that the two of you are creating.

Conflict: Can you handle it?

We somewhat touched upon this topic when we were discussing the aspect of learning to let go but conflict or the management of it is something we engage in everyday in all aspects of life. Conflict exists around us. Those who think that conflict is something you can avoid mitigate or somehow not deal with while living in a normal human society, please share the recipe!

In the context of marital boundaries, conflict is bound to happen. Again, at the risk of repeating myself, where there are two people living in close proximity, you are bound to have friction. No human is meant to glide through life without getting their feelings hurt or their emotions bashed up. Such is life and we better grow up and accept it. No matter how much you love, there are going to be times, when the two of you find attributes of the other person that just don't sit well with you. You get annoyed. Sometimes its feelings, emotions and thoughts that you have had to deal with in another situation in your life outside your marital realm that you have not been able to shed off. Those lingering thoughts, emotions and feelings become the silent fuel that will fire up the most dormant ignition in your private marital life.

You are human. First, don't be hard on yourself. Second, don't be hard on your spouse. They are human too. Conflicts will come and go but managing through them and dealing with the aftermath of the battlefield is something that we, sometimes, can do a better job off.

In my marriage, the biggest conflict situation was our extended families. Both our families. We both hailed from families that were just different. And I found it difficult to understand and accept his side of the family (in all honesty). And he found it difficult to understand and accept mine. We were both cordial and civil to our nemesis when the time came, but we made no attempt to extend that to love for them. And before you judge us harshly; neither did our individual families accept each of us with arms wide open. Every action has an equal and opposite reaction, right? Well, don't know how and when this reaction of mutual cordiality started, but it did.

I had always maintained that if my (ex) husband and I had been left alone on an island; we would have been just fine. But unfortunately, we didn't live in an island. We lived in real life with normal and real social interactions. Our families came to visit us from time to time. We had our normal social interactions of dinners, birthdays, family outings and holiday celebrations

197

together. But invariably, the air would be heavy with suppressed animosity and the interactions less than optimal. Either, he would get irritated with something my side of the family member said or did or I did with one of his.

But here is the more interesting thing. The families would eventually leave but we were left hanging on to those feelings. If he was irritated with mine, I would get upset. After all, it was my family. I grew up with them. I knew and understood what they meant and said. But he didn't. If it was his side of the family and I was upset with the family interaction, he was left feeling bad. He loved his family too. He was deeply engaged in the lives of each and every member of his side of the family. He wanted me to be a happily participating member of his family. I had some similar expectations. And both of us being relatively smart individuals, we knew what each other wants and expects. We also knew the kind of impact our interaction with the other's family left on our spouses. But, again, like mentioned before, we could not control our reactions. We had our reactions to the slightest of catalysts and we let the spark get out of hand. We lacked control of our reactions.

The situation would get even worse when we had some unfinished and unresolved conflict with our spouse flickering somewhere in our minds. The sparks would lead to forest fires before we knew it. And the impact then was even worse. Words were exchanged that left invisible marks and bruises that were brutal. And the reason the impact of these conflict situations were even more brutal is because the person on the other side knows you too well. He/she lives with you. They know where to hurt when the time comes. They know your Achilles heel just like you know theirs.

The love of your life also learns about you just as you learn about them. In this learning process, the education is not just restricted to the "good stuff" but also catalysts that can really hit a nerve.

And now, your love is not really your "team mate". Now they are the opposing side. You are in conflict...remember? Your brain is right now not focusing on things that bind you together. Right now all you can focus on is your enemy. And your enemy is...NOT your spouse. Trust me, sometimes it feels that ways. But they are not. Your enemy is your ego...your lack of ability to think through the situation clearly. But when did we say we were super humans? We are meant to be human and the connotations attached to that being screams loudly of irrational s. You will focus on your hurt emotions, your bruised feelings and your negative thoughts. And the more you focus on these burning emotions, feelings and thoughts; they take the form of your spouse. The poor human just happens to be the person in front of you whom you do not mind allowing the luxury of divulging your true thoughts and emotions to. And before you start feeling bad about your reaction, your spouse will do the exact same thing. That's what makes you human. That's what makes us animals.

So any textbook on conflict management will probably state, stay calm when you feel that fire just burning inside you. I say the same. When you feel that fire burning inside and you are ready to let the venom spew out, PULL BACK.

Words have a way of sticking to your memory. Be careful with them. You are not able to control your reaction right now. Understand that about yourself. You are overwhelmed with your feelings, emotions and thoughts that are not making you happy. If you can't control, don't react at all. Go completely silent. Do not speak when you are feeling the worst.

When your brain and your heart tells you to "make things right" by speaking out, STOP. That is probably the worst time to speak. You will speak in anger. You will not be utilizing the rational side of your brain. You cannot because you are wired to say things that are running through your head. That, my dear friend, is the perfect time to stay silent. When your brain and heart is screaming for you to scream, that is the time for you to stay quiet.

You must be thinking, "Easier said than done." Absolutely. It is easier to talk about it and very difficult to implement. But we are discussing is the art of dealing with difficult situations. You are in conflict and you know your reaction will peg to the illogical and irrational side of your brain. How about shutting down the system all together? Make a conscious effort to stop using your brain.

You might be able to do it but your spouse cannot. He/she is throwing nasty words and hurtful statements out towards you. How about letting them vent? You will be tempted to say something back, to correct the incorrect statements made or judgments passed. But no matter how much you want to speak up, ask yourself "Does this help?"

Saying anything in that situation will not. Both of you are in a position where you are not able to see the other person. You think you see the other person but all you see is the personification of the negative energy that you are not able to control. So stop trying to control. Just shut down the system. You will reboot later. You will re-start that computer again. But for now, just shut down.

Some might think that staying silent and controlled (shut down) is a sign of accepting defeat and agreeing to everything wrong that is being said about you. Some might think it's a sign of cowardice that you cannot speak up and set things right. Au contraire dear friend! You are accepting nothing. You have now shown more courage in letting that time pass. You will speak up but on your terms and at the right time. The right time for you. Hence you are going to be in control when you speak up. Staying silent is a self-control mechanism to stop yourself from reacting. You are now taking stock of your faculties to make sure that when the response does come out, you are the one who has a clear mind and controlled heart. The delivery of that response in that instance is far more superior.

But everything we have spoken about is the verbal conflict. (I am assuming that if you have any sort of physical conflict, you will know to get out of this relationship as soon as you can). The other side of conflict that is imperative for us to recognize and pay heed to the silent nonverbal conflict. "Now where did that come from? We don't have silent conflicts? We talk it out." Yes, that's probably true for ten percent of the conflict situations that you will deal with in marriage. The rest of the ninety percent is to deal with your own mind and thoughts.

By now, you probably know your spouse very well. You know their likes and dislikes, their thoughts and desires, whom they like and whom they don't. You are also keenly aware of the things that have been hinted at you about circumstances, events and

202

occasions where a scar was left on your spouse's psyche. You respect them and know not to instigate those situations to antagonize him/her.

To make your mind think about situations that you are probably dealing with but don't recognize it yet, let me show you an example.

If only the couple could be on an island, they would have a perfect life. Husband loves wife but finds it difficult to stay in close quarters with her mother. Mother of the bride stays in a different state. So, when she comes to visit, she is a house guest. For the first few times, the husband was somewhat tolerant. But soon it was evident that the husband didn't really have an affinity for his mum-in-law. The relationship between the husband and wife took a downward slide every time those visits happened. It wasn't as if the mother in law was doing anything. Let's just say that the husband and the mother were too similar in personality. Both were opinionated and didn't mind much sharing them. Both would let their judgments be known to those around.

Being the only child also made it difficult for the wife. She was always close to her mom. But now the most important person in her life couldn't really tolerate her mom being in the same quarters. Not that the husband had publicly aired his opinion about it. He was cordial and he was a good host. But the wife knew when things were amiss. And things became amiss when the home had her folks coming over. The unspoken stress in the air become palpable, the tension between the spouses became tangible and somehow the peace in the home vanished.

The poor wife was torn. She knew the reaction the household had to these visits and her interaction with her mum. But she couldn't just let her mom vanish from her life. She loved her husband but she also loved her mother. She wanted her folks to come and visit her new home but also knew the impact that those visits had on her life. She started becoming stressed at the thought of those visits even though she wanted her folks to come visit her. She also knew that even though her husband won't verbalize anything to her and was also verbally supportive to their visits, reality was something different. She felt distant from him during the time she had her folks over. The atmosphere at home was just strained. She didn't know what to do.

Nonverbal conflict sometimes can take more of a toll on your marriage than the ones that are aired out and fought out. The thoughts and emotions attached to them have far reaching consequences than the ones where you know where you and your spouse stand about a particular topic.

As you grow into a relationship, you are very quick to pick up the hot topics that you want to stay away from. In some case, you can't stay away because there are emotional tugs for you on those topics. That's where the real turmoil begins. Even though you know situations are going to make matters a little strained between you and your love, your heart or your sense of duty also pulls you towards those same situations. You feel torn and soon that feeling starts manifesting itself in your behavior either towards your spouse, or the other side or both.

The other horrible part of all this emotional tug-of-war is that while you are stuck in the middle, in most cases, the two sides that you are having to manage have no clue about the stress you are going through. They are so full of their own emotions and feelings towards each other that they are just "behaving normally." Hence, they are also under appreciative of the efforts you put in to keep peace at home.

The solution is simple. Detach yourself. I know it sounds far simpler than it can be in reality. But do me a favor and ask yourself. Whom are you trying to protect in the case above. The wife would be running from pillar to post to explain her mother's behavior to her husband and vice versa. The intent was not that the husband and the mother will become best friends. The idea was to protect each of their feelings from being hurt by the other side. But the wife's attempts were to protect adults who are more than capable of protecting themselves. Her husband and her mother did not need her protection.

Detaching yourself actually helps in protecting the only person who needs protection here. You. Or in the example, the wife. If you are the one stuck in the middle of this emotional rigmarole, you are the one who is going to need protection. If your husband is stressed, you will get hurt because the cause is your mother. If your mother's sensibilities are getting bruised, you are the one who bears the bruises because there are certain expectations from your spouse. Now, each of them probably has their rights to feel the way they are doing and they are within their rights also to express how they are feeling. It then falls on you to help yourself.

Imagine a situation like the example given about the spouses and the mother. A very common scenario in many households. When you become aware of the unspoken tension in the air, is it possible for you to distance yourself from the situation, at least mentally, if not physically.

I understand that what I am suggesting is far from being easy. In fact, it takes a lot of training of the mind to be able to achieve something like this with full success. But try it out. You might be surprised by the results.

The wife had to learn to do that. She had to verbally convey to her husband and her mother that the strain that they were feeling ultimately stresses her. She had to then convey to them that they had every right to feel the way they do but they couldn't express it in front of her, in no form or fashion. She was vehement when she proclaimed to them that she was the common link in the relationship. If they had positive or negative feelings, they needed to keep her out of it. She wouldn't entertain any comments either about her husband or her mother from the other side. Sometimes when she felt the air in the house was becoming heavy; she would take the car and go for a drive by herself. Her spouse and her mother were completely surprised that she would do such a thing but soon realized that they all needed the "time out". She needed to cool herself down and they needed to get that time to realize that the victim was not them but her.

Now, realize that these are simple examples for you to think about. As you start your marriage, this situation will be far-fetched. As you start the marital journey, everybody wants to get to know everybody else. Life is good! But life also catches up on you.

My simple advice will be try and pre-empt it as soon as you can. Set some ground rules (just like the wife did) from the get go. Save yourself from the mental and emotional torture before it starts. Right now, you might think that something like this will never happen to you and hopefully it never does but it is never too dumb to be well prepared.

Telling your loved ones that you love them is your prerogative! Telling them that love for one doesn't need to come at the cost of love for another is a perquisite! Telling yourself that adults need to be adults, is your duty to yourself! Telling yourself that you don't deserve to go through this emotional stress and strain is your right to happiness.

What surprised me somewhere in my life is how common this problem is for many a folks. At a mum's coffee meeting, one mother asked another about how things were with the in-laws (I have no idea how that topic started). But there is was, the mum was telling all of us how the spouses have now come to terms that some people are not meant to get along. She doesn't get along with her in-law family. This had caused a lot of strain in their marriage. But after ten years of being married (and a second marriage for both of them), they have now realized that them being married does not automatically imply that both sides of extended families have to be the best of buddies. She took the children to her folks' when she wants to. The father in turn takes the children to his folks' when he wants to. Or they visit when they individually want to see their loved ones. But they don't EXPECT their marital partners to comply with the happy visits anymore. But she also went on to say that it took a good ten years for them to come to terms with it. And it almost cost them their own marriage! Don't let it happen to you! You are starting a new partnership. And you also have an entity that you belonged to before you branched out on your own. The two don't have to mesh! The expectations are on your side and for you to manage. So manage it pro-actively versus reacting to the stress and tension. Take steps to let all adults around you know that you don't have expectations but also will not compromise on your happiness for the sake of their'. Detaching yourself to this extent is not ruled as "being selfish" or "not caring". If truth be told, you are being selfless and being very caring towards the ones that you love (in this case separately). It is because they can't get along, that you have had to be selfless and caring to their feelings to snap shut some of yours. And that's a message worth sharing with all concerned!

Who are you now... do you recognize yourself?

Ask any married individual (less than three years) this question. I have a feeling a majority of them will smile and say it's lovely to have lost themselves in the love they have found. They have the dreamy eyes and the lovely aura of "we are still like newly-weds". You probably have that same aura right now. You should cherish this feeling. It's exquisite! The two of you are entrenched in the knowledge that you are gaining about each other. You thought you knew your love before but now you are getting to know him as one. The two of you are one now. You are getting to know the nice and not so nice aspects of each other. You start reflecting on each other's thoughts, likes and dislikes. If you have heard or seen your partner like or dislike something or someone, you were learning and processing. Your brain is slowly processing the life of togetherness. Your brain is also learning how to live in this new entity as one. And the feeling is amazing.

Now go ahead and ask the same question to somebody who has been married for five years or more. You will realize that the reaction you receive is slightly different. Individuals grimace and say "Yeah! It's lovely. We are married and love each other." But you can soon sense that the individual is expressing something else without really saying it. I won't be surprised if you sense something is amiss. The couple is still in love. They are still together and work great as an entity but somewhere there is a want that is dying to be spoken but words are not found. The individual probably thinks that if they truly express themselves anymore, he or she will raise eyes brows. People don't like going against normal social norms. You love, you marry and then you behave in a certain manner. Well, the individual is conforming to that social norm.

But if the person is a really good friend or one who is not afraid to voice their true feelings, ask them where that individual now exists in that marriage. You might be surprised at the truth once the flood gates open. As much as individuals love the feeling of losing themselves in the love that they find around them, as time goes by, they also crave to be who they are as an individual. Somewhere someone is lost in a union.

Mind you, every common sense advises that you should get lost in this new entity that you have entered. It should become the identity that you carry. It is you! But our individuality sometimes stems out and craves to breath a couple of gasps now and then.

A friend of mine had been married for almost ten years. A beautiful, relatively tranquil marriage. Have a child, beautiful home, blossoming careers and well planned retirement being furnished and staged. PTA meetings, swim and tennis classes for the youngster, occasional cookouts, wonderful parties for neighbors and friends and wonderful home for the family kept them all engaged. They were a normal family with their very normal love and feuds to run the course of life.

She had to take a business meeting to New York once. She had visited New York City hundreds of times before for business and pleasure. This time though things were different. She needed a break from everything happening in office and at home. She was ready to give New York an opportunity and her in it. Her usual business meetings meant airports, meeting rooms, lunch meetings and then room service for her to relax and get ready for the next day. This time she wanted to get out and get to know a little bit more of New York by herself. She allowed herself to join the rest of her colleagues for dinner and plans thereafter. And yes, her colleagues were also surprised that she would join them.

During dinner she realized that her team held a certain opinion of her. She was deemed as a little hardnosed, very capable and yet a little difficult to get to know. She accepted that. It was her professional persona that she wanted to sustain. But simultaneously she also allowed herself to relax and enjoy the dinner and dance thereafter. But more than her colleagues, she surprised herself. She was back to being her twenty something self when she worked hard but also played hard. She was back to being able to put the home and office aside for some time and enjoy the ambiance and the music. She danced just like she used to. She enjoyed the evening for the pure- hearted fun just like she used to. She was herself again.

And that's when she realized that she had completely forgotten about her. She had done everything by the books. She worked hard to get her professional status and also worked hard in her personal life. She fell in love and married the man of her dreams. They had worked hard to make a life for themselves. A house, child, country club memberships, golf, friends and family security. But beneath all the layers of professional and personal complications that had found its way into her life, she had forgotten about her free self. She was always a hard working person. But she also knew how to enjoy life. She would go out and relax with a drink or two. She would enjoy the music and the dance. She enjoyed being free. And today she was back to her own self outside the layers and she was shocked.

Her shock was not that life had caught up to her but more at the subtle way it did it. Somewhere in time, she had lost touch with some of the things that rejuvenated her. Somewhere in time, she had evolved into being another self but one who lived a life for her profession and her home. But who was she now. She didn't recognize herself as the stuck up person that she was finding herself to be. She wasn't the person who would simply run from pillar to post making it in time for the parents-teacher meetings and for the swim lessons. She used to be fun. How come she wasn't fun anymore? Her child didn't know her as fun. Her love and she would get into the occasional verbal strains where it was very evident that she was turning into a control freak. Who was she now? She wasn't meant to be the one who frets about the house being picture perfect, her parties to be the talk of the town, her child to be the best possible swimmer in his division, her career to accelerate to its optimal way and her life to be how it was. She loved what they had achieved but she didn't realize that somewhere in that process, she had completely lost track of the person she was becoming.

After coming back from New York, she also felt a little guilty. Though she had behaved in the most respectable manner, she felt guilty about allowing herself to have realized and seen what she was missing. I think she felt most guilty about the fact that she enjoyed herself and missed that light hearted side of herself. She was guilty that she was deviating from the persona she had built around her marital self. But when had she planned to have this marital persona in the first place?

Yes, as much as we enjoy this beautiful ride that we call marriage, we also simultaneously develop our marital personality. But somewhere out there is also your own personality that needs to come out and enjoy the sunlight once in a while. You must be thinking this woman is asking for too much now. How does one keep the individual personality and develop a marital entity simultaneously? Who has the time? It will be what it will be?

Here is the risk of not paying attention to your true self: you will one day wake up in New York and start looking at the life that had you encompassed and start questioning everything. More so you will realize that your child, your spouse and your colleagues know you only for the person you have evolved to but not the whole you. You will miss the things that give you the fresh energy to take on more challenges in life. You will stop recognizing yourself.

My sincere advice is not to let this happen to you. Keep that free self-inside you- ALIVE. That side of you doesn't need to stay with you all the time. You don't need that free you to be standing side by side in everything you need to do to go ahead with the marital bond you are developing. But once in a while, you do need that

215

free side to breathe some fresh air, come out and remind you that you exist as an individual too. More than you, your spouse and future family will need to see that side of you. They need to know and remind themselves who you truly were before life happened. And you need to see that side of your spouse. You might be completely amazed how refreshing you will find that free side for the two of you to your marital harmony.

My friend used to enjoy dancing and music, a night out with friends and free spirited banter with friends. She could have walked through the same successful walk of life but sometimes allowed herself to just "chill out". An occasional night out with friends and hubby to enjoy the night life of Chicago, New York or LA wouldn't have taken away anything from her marital life. It would have reminded her husband of how truly free she was.

Staying true to yourself is very important for sustenance in your marital entity that you are building. As you start off, stay true to your likes and wants. Do you want to go out and enjoy comedy central, a play on occasions, a good book club, a flirty night with your girl-friends or just a night out watching adult films? Why don't you do that now? Don't blame it on marriage. Your spouse did not put conditions on this marriage (at least I hope not). It's all in your mind.

You are the one who can and will stop yourself from letting that free self-come out and breathe once in a while. You probably haven't seen your mother free and spirited about things that made her and only her happy. You always saw your mother taking care of the family first. And that's all you wanted. You wanted to be taken care off. Then you saw all the women around your neighborhood that did the same. Conditioning 101. And then of course you have all your other friends also doing the same. They too abide by the social norms that somehow have morphed into telling us not to be ourselves. Be the self that the society wants to see you as. Society has managed to encode in our DNA the kind of person it wants to see when we are married. You behave a certain way, you are a certain way and you expect certain things. That's when you are a good society participant. Otherwise you are ...well, you are just different!

I will say, it's ok to be different but be you. Enhance the side of you that brings the smile on your face. Your family needs that smile and your spouse needs that smile. You need the smile when it comes straight from the heart. Yes, those cookouts and the PTA meetings also bring smiles but be honest with yourself.

Keep yourself happy. If you can make small little deviations to the plan to get the free side out and breathing, do it. It will allow your smile to be more genuine. And yes my friend, year later when you look back, you will still recognize yourself. You will be able to show the true side of you in its wholeness to your spouse and your family.

I hope you realize that I keep mentioning family here. There is a reason for it. Sometime in the future, you will want to have a family of your own. When the young one(s) come into your life, conditioning takes over again and we almost become "wanna be parents". All the kiddos really want is to see the real side of you. The true side. That's what they connect with the best. But we will save the more mature side of this topic for a later day. For now, ladies and gentlemen, we still have a marriage to get fully ready for!

There are things you do not like about your spouse?

As you read this topic, you must think "what an outrageous thing to say?" It is. You have found this person who seems to walk on water. You have fallen in love and you are going to start a life with this person. You love everything about them. Everything!

The only problem is you don't know EVERYTHING!

Some of you might have lived with your spouse before deciding to check the box on walking down the aisle bit. Others might be the epitome of "love at first sight". You met, fell in love and knew that this was it. The rest of us lie somewhere in between. But no matter where you lie on this scale of "knowing the love of your life", you really don't know them till you have tied yourself to "together forever".

As you start the journey with the mindset that this is the person you will spend your old age with, your 401(k) with, your old age hospital visits with, your brain starts configuring a whole new set of data. Your expectations from this person rise notches above when you were still in your evaluation phase. You now have a life to live with this one person. And your poor heart and brain starts expecting things. Even if they don't expect, they know what they don't want. And many of those things that you don't want start taking shape.

Here are a few common things that people start relating to their close ones after years of their marriage about the love of their life-

1. Doesn't open the door anymore for me

2. Doesn't help me with the kitchen

3. Why do I have to clean up after him?

4. Is not focused on his career as he should be right now

5. Is focused too much on his career all the time

6. Is making decisions without consulting me

7. Or, can't make even the simplest of decisions without asking me

8. He doesn't care about my career

9. Farts!

On one side of the spectrum to

1. She is anal about certain things. Everything has to be a certain way

2. She wants to eat out all the time

3. She is complaining about the same things that she used to like about me at one point

4. She is a spender. We can't afford that

5. She is not taking care of herself anymore. She has put on weight

6. She doesn't understand the nature of my work

7. She doesn't care about my career

8. She agrees with everything I say. I just don't know what she is truly thinking

9. We have too many arguments

10. We don't argue as much!

11. She NAGS!

It happens to all couples. And there is nothing wrong with it. And just when you smile to yourself and think "Oh, then that's ok", let me carry on by saying "it only gets worse as time goes by". Yes, it does. Children happen, life happens and both of you EVOLVE. You both change from the person you once used to be. So just be prepared!

If you draw up a list of all the factors why this one person made your heart skip a beat, your cheek flush and your thoughts run towards "happily ever after", you will know why you said yes to the walk down the aisle. That list is one that you should probably keep handy for future. Somewhere in your bed side table, hidden in your closet under your clothes or under the bathroom sink! Anywhere but keep it handy. You will need it and you should keep looking at it time and again to remind yourself of your decision making factors. God knows you will wonder sometimes- "what the hell was I thinking?"

You see, life has a way of catching up. Yes, I know, I have probably said it a zillion times to you already, but it is absolutely true. Life happens. You don't know how it sneaks up on you. After marriage, you enjoy the newness factor of being a couple, being viewed as a couple, being in love and being in a new life. And then the newness factor wears off. You start getting used to it. You start getting used to the love that you have now surrounded yourself with. You are slowly getting used to the new life. The excitement has now translated into nothing but LIFE!

So, all this time, your focus was directed on the things that were happening to you. You had "bigger fish to fry" as they say. Now the fish is already fried. You channel that focus on other things. Your eyes and brain are seeking things where that energy and focus can be directed. And all that you see is not good. Suddenly, you start seeing things that were probably always there, but just in the background and you didn't notice. Suddenly, the smallest things start getting to you. And as humans, the small things don't usually come under the "good" category. They are usually things that we feel need some attention and improvement.

Addressing this is as some say somewhat of "a sticky wicket". You don't really have any control over your likes and dislikes. It's just the way you feel. And you shouldn't have to tip-toe around your likes/dislikes all the time. By the same token, your spouse shouldn't have to live life on your terms. That's not fair on them either. If they like being a little bit untidy at home (they have to be their organized best in office all the time), they are entitled to do so. After all they are at home, where they can afford to be as relaxed as they want to be. It's their home too. Or if your spouse wants to be anal about the décor of the house and keep the living room decorated to make Martha Stewart proud, they have a right to that. After all, it's their home too. So, where do you draw the line between keeping your sanity and letting your spouse have their space?

You don't and you really can't! What you can do is make those lists. Hopefully you already have the list of the things about your spouse, you fell in love with. Keep referring to them. On a rainy day while having a wonderful cup of espresso relaxing on the bed, share that list with your spouse. Bring the knowing smiles back.

But also make a list of the things that are now getting on your nerves. We all get educated but it is funny how little we use our education for the simple things. Humans can build spaceships but we cannot list simple things that can either make us happy or sad. Penning those down (assuming you still use a pen) or typing it up (which is where most of the world is directed to now); will help you clear your head first. And that's where you need to start... your head. Again, at the risk of sounding like a broken record, you have better control of yourself versus what you have over others.

List down the things that are making you cringe. Identifying them will help them be clear in your head. Also it avoids you from generalizing. It used to happen to me all the time. My husband had the habit of not closing closet doors behind him. For some reason, that would get to me and get to me bad! So, when the outburst came after bottling it up for long, the words were more to the tune of "You never finish anything. You are incapable of tying up loose ends and really seeing things through. How the hell will you be able to manage this task for me?" All he had done was volunteer to take care of the broken closet door for us to relieve me of the stress of having to manage the work. But years of bottled up anger towards the door somehow came across in terms that really left a scar on him! Unnecessary! In my defense, the closet door was probably damaged because it wasn't shut properly all the time! But the delivery of that angst was horrible! Of course, he did follow through and did complete all tasks. But somehow my accusation was aimed as a habitual statement versus a statement of fact.

Your statement of fact list will first get your brain to think clearly about what exactly bothers you. What about your spouse do you see that you really don't like right now. (If at all possible, make that list short and sweet, will you? I am sure you know why I say that.)

Now consider taking one of those cozy, near the fireplace, cuddled with a glass of warm red wine moments of your life. Both of you are relaxed and truly in the mood to be listening to each other. Take that occasion to sit with that list (hopefully both of you) and exchange it. Have a few laughs about it. Tease each other just like you used to when you were dating. But do reveal your true thoughts to them such that they know. You are truly in no place to expect them to change all that just because you don't agree with them. But the next time they do something that bothers you, you guys might have a laugh or exchange a few knowing looks across the room about it. Acknowledgement helps. Acknowledgement is the first step towards working things out.

When I got informed that I had become anal about the house cleanliness and was becoming somewhat nagging, I realized that I was turning into my MOTHER! She would drive us crazy about putting things back in the right place and keeping the house picture perfect. And as much as I hated her being on my case about this cleanliness factor, I was now doing the same to my household. And I acknowledged it. It actually helped me, knowing that no matter how much I fight the fact that I disliked the way she nagged me about it, I was now nagging somebody else to do the same things. It didn't do me much good in correcting it. The damage was already done and the DNA had taken over this poor mortal but at least I knew that the problem was with me and not with those around me. And hopefully you are asking me, "So, what did you do after you found out and acknowledged?" Nothing! Along with the acknowledgement, I also had acceptance. I was accepting that I was turning into my mother. What that allowed me to do was turn that into a family joke. Every time I "nagged" about the cleanliness around the house, I would joke with my spouse about how horrible it sounds. How it helped was to bring some level of recognition to his dislike for this side of me. At least I acknowledged that I am being obnoxious. It actually brought an occasional smile to his face.

Admitting that you can have faults will help you understand that so can your spouse. And talking or making jest of these faults is not only human but also helps the other side understand that you acknowledge, accept and if under your control, might try to be a little bit more sensitive to it. That small gesture goes a mile.

So what if your spouse passes gas on occasions. Human body was never declared as the perfect machine. So your spouse is falling prey to the mechanical failures of a wonderfully designed machine. A fault that if they are given a choice, I am positive, they themselves would like to avoid. But are you really going to hold that against them? Is it not enough that they might hold it against themselves at times? Now being obnoxious about the process of passing gas might be a different ball game all together.

At times when you are ready to blow your lid off, you might use the lovely list that actually brought the two of you together. At times when you are in your more controlled and happy mode, use the list that gets yours blood boiling. Make it a two way process.

With each of you admitting something nasty about the other person, the impact might be slightly blunted. (The use of alcohol and nice romantic setting is also advised to mellow down the blow but I will leave it to your discretion.) Sharing a laugh about the nasty list helps you understand the hot buttons with each other too. So the more positive spin you can give to the situation, the better for you.

Now, let's talk about the frequency with which the list should be created and shared. For those of you who are wide eyed at the need for more than one list, news flash for you is that "The list is also ever evolving." Things that your spouse does today which might be considered slightly irritating, might completely go away tomorrow and they might pick up another nasty habit. For all you know, they might actually pay heed to your list and work on some of the items on the list to make you happy. But that doesn't mean that your woes have all come to an end. Au-contraire, my dear! That list will take a life of its own. It will evolve as the two of you grow older together for the happily ever after.

Other habits that your spouse starts engendering slowly take their own place in your list. And I am sure you would have contributed to populating the list created by your spouse. Try keeping it fresh and small. Try keeping it prioritized and necessary. Please don't consider placing items on the list just to jab at your spouse. This is neither the forum nor the method to do so. The idea is to solve a situation not create one with these lists!

But as needed, your list also needs to be shared with your love. You will know when to share the next list or the two of you can set a tentative timeline when you guys think you need to relieve the stress and have a few laughs. But laugh you must. Having a sense of humor about such things is a catalyst to making these solutions work. If you can't laugh at yourself and take a punch or two from the person closest to you, you are ill-prepared to share your   list.

Now, the part you have to be careful about is if you or your spouse start using this list a bit too frequently or if you find that the list is slowly increasing in its population set. Then, it might be time to take a pause. If there are too many things that are getting on one or both of your nerves about each other, maybe it's time to have a different conversation. In that case, the problem might not be rooted in simple little habitual items that are just bothering you but something more deep rooted that you or your spouse is not able to vocalize. Maybe you or they need some help in thinking through some more fundamental root-causes that is behind this situation? Maybe it's time to relook at the list you had made which tells you why this person was so special for you.

Weighing the bigger priorities (like the list that made you happy enough to say YES) against the ones that now makes you question your decision (like the ones on the nasty list you keep looking at) is also important. That nasty list is just symbolic of your own greed. Now you want it all. But you have to be honest with yourself. If the items on the list are truly that important to you that you will risk more fundamental items for it, then maybe you needed to see this side of your spouse before making the decision.

But for those of you who find that list has items that are things that you get irate about but if push comes to shove you are ready to live with, and then learn to live with it. Make that list work for you. That list is never going to be perfect for you. But neither are you that perfect, are you? As much as we love to believe that we are, we have to accept that these lists are a mixed bag. That's why there is always retail therapy.

So as you start your journey of getting to know your spouse a little better every day:

1. Keep the happy list handy

2. Keep the nasty list ready

3. Have the occasional date to air some dirty laundry

4. Learn to take a joke about yourself (yes, you are not perfect either)

5. Learn to express to your love that yes, they are human too but you love them just the way they are (only with a few slight tweaks!)

You will look for others to blame

While we discussed the topic that you might learn new things about your spouse as your walk through the journey of life, we conveniently missed the side where you might discover aspects that are in your new marital environment that you don't like. As hard as sometimes it might be for us to imagine, marital harmony doesn't always generate from only the two people concerned, but also from the social fabric that we find ourselves in as a couple.

We marry an individual, but more often than not, get married to a whole new family, a new group of friends, and a whole new group of neighbors and sometimes even a new city or country! There is a lot to take in. And unlike the stories that usually end in "happily ever after", the world doesn't stop revolving right after the wedding bells ringing. .

And just like things you learn about your spouse, you also learn new things about the social fabric you have now entered. You learn about your newly acquired social environment. This social fabric is made interesting by the new family that you have now entered. A group of (adults for the most part) whom now you adopt as one of your own.

For some very lucky individuals, it is very easy or should I say "made" very easy. The newly adopted family is so lovely that you have a natural affinity for them. You love them as if they were your own. You look forward to having them over or to going over to their place. You look forward to meeting them in gatherings and exchanging updates with them.

For some lesser mortals, life is not always so smooth. You DO not get along with your martially adopted family, you DO not look forward to having them over and you want to avoid any gatherings where you have to come across them at all. But for the sake of your love, you keep the chilly smile and count the hours. But that irritation inside you keeps boiling and churning till it reaches a point where you can't take it anymore. But you don't have the words to express to your spouse that you would much rather keep your distance. After all, isn't there a saying that distance makes the heart grow fonder. Well, you can at least try?

But your words desert you. You don't have the heart to hurt your love. Instead you let the heat simmer inside of you. You tolerate the social gatherings. But, there is a limit to your own patience. Everyone has limits.

When my friend was getting married to his very pretty lady love, all he could see were the stars and the sky. Reality hit home a little later when he fully comprehended the meaning of having her doting love for her elder sister. His lady love was a doting wife and also a doting daughter, sister and daughter-in-law. Life couldn't be better. The only problem is that when my friend was sprinting towards the "happily ever after", he didn't realize that it will be crowded. Soon after his marriage, the realization did sink in or should I say was thrust upon him. He almost felt that there were three of them in the marriage. His unmarried sister (by marriage) was always there in their marital circle. She was there to help with the home, there to help with the furniture, there to help with the move, the selection of the fabric, how they should save, when they should save, why retirement planning was so important for them and also what food they should eat to avoid early utilization of their life insurance policies (Oh, did I forget to mention that they also needed life insurance policies from the get go?). She meant well and that's what he kept telling himself.

He knew his new wife had always consulted her sister on everything about life. She looked upon her elder sister as her second mother. The sisterly love between the two was almost endearing. Well, almost. He didn't realize that it was a "buy one get one free" deal that he was signing up for. And what looked like a lot of help started feeling like claustrophobia soon thereafter. All he wanted was to be with his wife, to make decisions where the two of them get together and to spend a life where they could breathe easy without somebody breathing down their necks.

The fact that his wife got married before her elder sister could get hitched also weighed upon their marriage. It seemed like his wife was almost apologetic for having taken the plunge before her all-controlling sister could settle down.

But the existence of the third person in the marriage was getting to my friend. He was claustrophobic. But unfortunately, he couldn't have an adult conversation about this problem with his wife. He knew how close she was to her sister and how hurt she will be if anything was aired against her. But the care and protectiveness about his wife could not stop this young man from feeling bottled up and angry. The anger was soon reaching a point where the venom was starting to spill.

On visits, he made it very obvious that the sister's opinions were discarded and not accepted. It didn't matter if the suggestions were about furniture or a movie to watch, he pushed back. And not in a nice and gentle manner either. He would be nasty about his displeasure with her suggestions. He became sarcastic about comments that the sister aired during visits. He resisted plans of visiting the sister whenever his wife suggested. He became practically rude to the sister on any given occasion.

Now, this gentleman was one of very good upbringing. He was known to be a gentleman in all settings. Hence, this behavioral change was a surprise to all around him. Especially his wife. She didn't know what had come over him. He was always so generous and gracious around everybody but not around "her family". See, the problem was the she could not differentiate between the impact of her family and that of her sister. For her they were all the same. So, you can imagine the impact this change in attitude and behavior was having on her. She loved her family and she loved her husband but for some reason the two sides of her life was not coming together harmoniously. And she was distraught.

For her, the only factor that was causing the negativity in her life was her husband's reactions. That made things even worse for her. She loved him too much to think badly about him but his behavior around her family was obviously RUDE!

Needless to say, this unspoken strain created a rift between the husband and wife and took a toll on their marriage.

My poor friend couldn't fathom how his wife couldn't see that her sister was domineering and overbearing. His poor wife couldn't fathom why her husband was so antagonistic towards her family.

Whenever they spoke about this (supposedly nonexistent) eight hundred pound gorilla in the room, the conversations were usually right after a visit by the sister or a phone call with her. Hence the emotions had already entered the system and clouded any rationale and controlled strain of conversation. They would end up fighting about irrelevant topic but never brought up the one thing that mattered... it was THEIR marriage.

My friend was trying to paint his sister in law into a monster. Everything was her fault. If his wife made a wrong decision about the restaurant they wanted to go to, it was the fault of the sister-in-law. "She must have suggested it." If his wife wanted to go to Paris instead of Cancun for their vacations, it was the fault of the sister in law. "She must have suggested Paris. I have heard her mention it twice already while talking to you." Soon, he was discrediting his wife of making any sane and mature decisions. According to him, his wife was slowly becoming incapable of making any independent decisions. According to him, she was always influenced, manipulated and guided by her sister. Hence, all decisions were colored by the lenses of "I don't like them".

The poor wife didn't know how to cleanse him off his thinking. Also, though she knew that her sister was the one with the stronger personality, she couldn't ask her to stay out of her life. After all, that was HER sister!

Their marriage was falling apart. He complained that there was one too many people in the marriage. She complained that he was just nasty. Soon the love that got them together was taking a back seat.

It is amazing how many folks, if they are truly honest with you, will admit that they had CROWDED marriages. Neither spouses wanted it nor did the external crowd realize that they were a burden to somebody else's life. But guess what, it happens all the time! When our loved ones don't know how to let go of situations, this happens all the time.

Can I first stop and see what would you do in such a situation? Would you turn to the wife and ask her to stop being a child? Or would you turn to my friend, the husband, and ask him to give her the benefit of the doubt that she was not biased?

Ideally, it would be sensible for the sister to realize that she needs to back off. But that's too much to ask. If she did have the senses, then this situation might have been avoided all together. But such is not the case. In the marriage, it is sometimes as difficult to talk to each other as it is to talk to others. It didn't help that the couple were also unable to talk about this situation without getting emotionally charged.

Here are a few things that could have helped the situation:

1. The husband talks to the wife to express his true and unadulterated feelings. Factual statements always help. In this situation, the wife would then have to take the ball and run with it. As you can imagine, it won't be a fun task. She has to shed the inertia of habit that she has formed throughout her life. She will also have to become conscious of her role in making her husband comfortable.

2. The wife then has to make a judgment call. Does she bring her sister into this conversation topic separately or not? She has to be aware of the sensitivity of the situation for her sister. It wasn't her fault in the first place. She was made to feel as if nothing had changed and she went about behaving accordingly. Her only fault was that she herself should have taken steps back after the marriage.

3. The wife then has the majority of the work to do. She has to come to terms with the fact that the marriage is for two people and two people only. She can't continue to lead life as if she was still the baby girl of her house where her

sister comes and tells her what to do. She has to take charge

4. In the process, the wife now also risks hurting the feelings of her sister. After all, she didn't just barge in; she was allowed in to create this situation. So, imagine the shock when the doors now get shut? But the wife has to be cognizant of the fact that her sister is a mature adult. Even if she gets hurt, she has to take the bitter pill and move on. Again, the sister wouldn't want her marriage to be destroyed either. It is the wife's duty to fully comprehend that they are all adults in this situation.

In these sticky, emotionally charged situations involving others, it becomes very easy for the spouses to try and place the blame on somebody else. In the example shared, my friend was using the sister as his scape goat. In reality, the responsibility of the marriage is on the two of them; the two people in the marriage. It is very convenient to start blaming others and seeking targets for the finger pointing. He had to realize that the sister was doing things out of the goodness of her heart, trying to help her baby sister. She didn't deserve to be treated badly or disrespectfully.

Yes, she should have had the sense to back off after the wedding but there is very little one can do to control the actions of others.

On the other hand, had my friend taken charge of the conversation and made his wife aware of his real thoughts, in a calm and collected manner, the situation might have been nipped in the bud. But then again, you live, experience and learn.

But for many of you, it will be very helpful to realize that marriage is meant for two people. Society then makes it about everybody else. Families get involved, friends get involved and careers get involved. If the two people getting married keep their eye on the ball and stay focused on each other, all external matters become much easier to handle and tackle when the need arises.

Unfortunately for many, this realization takes place years into the marriage and by that time the damage is done and the impact is irreversible. Many a times, at a much later stage, even the surrounding families or friends realize the damage done to the marriage but more often than not, it is too late. By the time, they back off, or the couple decides to re-shuffle their tactics in managing the situation, the impact is already done and the couple grows apart. They either have given up fighting for the marriage or they give up on each other completely. Either way, it is far too late.

Hence, instead of looking for scape goats for your marriage just be ruthlessly protective about your marriage. It is yours to cherish and to keep. Others come and go. They have their own lives to live. If those around you get hurt or abraded by the sudden change in your attitude towards then (in the process of protecting your marriage), so be it. Either they will come around or time will be a very useful healing tool, but the marriage needs protection.

And yes, the only two people who can protect the marriage are the two people in it.

You look at other couples and want to be them

How many times have you looked at somebody else and said 'I wish I looked like her" or "I wish I was him". Oh, do be honest. Everybody thinks those words at some point in their lives. For those of you either contemplating marriage or just married, you will do the exact same thing. The only difference, you will start looking at other couples and think "wish we were like them". And yes, the opposite also happens. You also look at some couples and think "God forbid we ever become like them". Either way our brains are in the mode of continuous evaluation of others and comparing it to what you have.

As juvenile as it sometimes sound, you might be amazed at how often one spouse complains to the other about comparing their partnership to those of others.

As couples, you will find your social avenues. You will meet different people and different couples in different settings. More often than not, you meet a new pair and say "wow, how happy they look." What we don't realize is that at that very moment, our brain has just processed a different set of words. It is registering it as one of the following items

    1.   Do we look as happy as they do?

2. Why are we not as happy as them?

3. Wish I had what they have

4. What do they have and how come we don't?

But we are always in denial. We won't admit it to ourselves that the configuration of the words was different in our minds than what gets spelled out. But our spouse does. When we make the lethal mistake of saying those god forsaken words in front of the spouses, the set of words that runs through theirs is

1. My love is not happy with me

2. There is a deficiency in my love

3. There is a deficiency in me. I am not able to fulfil him/her

4. There is something wrong with our marriage

5. My spouse is never happy, no matter how much I try

Looking at all those words spelled out, many of us will have wide eyes. How did "how happy THEY look" get translated to so many different interpretations? And here lies the beauty of the human brain, my friend.

We are born to be jealous. We, like other animal species, like to have our territory marked out with no encroachment. But unfortunately for us, we don't live in caves and don't have the luxury of seclusion from other couples. We run into them and as we do, we also compare and contrast "us" with "them". Unfortunately, this is especially true for women. Women are always seeking perfection and how else are they going to attain that without realizing what is amiss? (Or that's what we like to tell ourselves)

When we meet random couples, we are comparing and contrasting our relationship with theirs. How they laugh, how they hold each other's hands, how much of a public exhibition do they put up about their love for each other is all in question. And we don't stop there. We extend it to then contrasting it with how we laugh; how we hold each other's hands and how do we look in public. It happens almost naturally. It happens more when we see couples who look happier than you do.

Now, here comes the word of caution. Not all that you see is true. Or maybe all that you see is not where the story stops. Couples who look happy and cozy are sometimes the ones who are going through the most turmoil. We get taught in our lives that don't believe all that you see but we never really pay heed to all that we are taught, do we? Every household has a story to tell. We never stop and ask. We simply take what we see and make our own assumptions with it.

As you start this journey of marital bliss, you will most probably fall prey to this game too. You will look at other couples and wish your togetherness was like theirs. First and foremost, that is not going to help you in any form or fashion. Of course, you can't stop your brain from thinking or wishing. But try and stipulate one statement after the thought has made its journey. "What is their story?"

When we have our hard days in marriage (yes, you will have them too), we become even more susceptible to the comparing and contrasting game. We are so busy trying to see what is wrong with us, that we seek the answer in others. But two things to keep in mind at that turbulent point:

1. They are two individuals who are completely different from you and yours truly. There is a reason why they are together and the two of you are with each other. The chemistry and configuration of their relationship is completely different than what you have with yours.

2. The second aspect is that you don't know what is truly happening behind the façade that you see. They might be the truly happy couple that they seem to be or they might

246

have their own set of problems that you are clueless about. These problems don't have to be similar to those of yours. They could be completely different than the ones that you think you have with your marriage. But problems they are and two individuals have to deal with them.

We, as humans, are always judging books by their covers. We are very quick to decide how happy, sad, successful, literate or civilized people are by simply looking at the way they are dressed, how they behave, their skin color or their facial demeanor. We might try to deny it but we are all prejudiced before we are not! The case is no different when it comes to couples. As an entity you are sending strong messages too when you meet other people. The only difference is that those looking at you now are thinking of you as "they".

"They look happy" or "they seem so comfortable" or "they look snug" or "love the way they look at each other". Those "they" statements are always in the air when we meet those outside the "they".

After making the first mistake of assuming that what you see is the reality, we then make the second mistake. We poke our supposed true findings to our spouse. Our partner might have not noticed all the "they" statements that you ran through your head. But you make the simple mistake of letting them in your thoughts which are there in the first place, because today was not your happy day!

On the drive back from the excellent party you just attended, you make the offhand comment about "did you notice how happy they looked", or "do you know how adorably they were kissing each other at any given opportunity?" We tell ourselves that we are having a common conversation. But are we? In all honesty, we also take these opportunities to convey a certain message to our partner about what we find endearing to us.

Not only did we not stop to validate if what we saw was the whole story or not, we also extend our spouse the courtesy of thinking that they are inadequate. We know that we didn't mean to but we do. We could have simply said "being in the crappy mood I am in, I was finding ways of evaluating all the other couples around me. Everybody looked happier than I was. Remind me again how do we look when we are happy?"

A simple turn of focus from "they" to "us" helps two folds. Not only are you conveying to your spouse that you are happy overall with him/her but just having a bad day, but also the fact that you were merely judging others for the sake of judging. Your spouse is not going to feel as if your relationship is being compared or contrasted against. And they will definitely not feel that they can't make you happy because you just told them that "we are happy".

It truly is as simple as that but very difficult to keep in mind when we are having those bad days. But give it a try. Tell yourself first that the day hasn't been your best. Remind yourself that tomorrow is yet another day and yesterday was beautiful. Then consider vocalizing for both of you that you are happy. You are having one of those bad days which makes the happy ones seem distant and far but "this too shall pass". Tomorrow seriously is another day!

Communication issues

How many times have you heard married couple say that they have a communication gap? Well, almost never. You see, we are of the strong belief that if we are together in the "happily ever after" mode we are perfectly synched in. Then, how can we have communication gaps? And if we do, then shouldn't we be better off being separated than together. After all, how can you be together and have communication issues?

You see, humans mastered the art and science of languages but in the process also mastered the art of making simple sentences very complicated. (That's how we designed a very complex and successful profession called the legal system.) We first learned how to speak and then somewhere in the process realized that what we say is not what the brain actually registers. So, then we had to tell each other how to understand what we are saying. We call it interpretation!

How we want to deliver our thoughts via words and how it finally gets interpreted might be miles apart. Somewhere in the process of coding, delivering and de-coding, words have a way of finding a life of their own. And the brain has a field day with it. And we call it miscommunication!

Let me exhibit to you one simple example from my life. At an early stage of my career, a colleague of mine flaunted his now accumulated (over twenty years of career) financial security to me. He was sharing how he had started saving when he was very young, had lived frugally and managed to go way over and beyond his retirement target. While he was flaunting, all I was registering was that he had already reached his retirement status, how his position might open up for grabs someday soon and what strategies I need to learn from him to go above and beyond my retirement target. Thereafter, coming back home, I relayed the conversation back to my spouse. And left it as facts without stating my take-away from the conversation. Years later, my husband begrudgingly admitted that he felt slighted and insulted at the tone of that particular conversation. He claimed he had every right to feel so since my words left him with the impression that he wasn't doing enough for me in our marriage. He felt that I was somehow insecure about our financial status and that I was somehow taken in by the gentleman because of my show of respect for him for having achieved his goals. All I asked myself was, how in God's name did I manage to convey this message to him?

Such is the power of words!

In marriage, our words can come back to bite us. What makes the bite even more pronounced is that the gap between the words and the thoughts are like a playfield for devils in action. And oh by the way, those bites usually come in installments...sometime much later in life when you are least expecting them.

At this stage of your life, as you are starting this new chapter, one very important thing to keep in mind about communicating with your spouse is that "do it". But do it in simple and clear terms. And as you receive the communication, if you don't like what you hear or say, clarify! Ask your spouse and yourself if the interpretation was synched with the intention? What have you got to lose by asking this simple question?

Clarifications sought today will save both of you some pain today and tomorrow. Why not risk it? Don't rely on the way your brain is decoding the message being forwarded, all the time. If you heard or saw something that makes you cringe, hurts you or questions your partner's intentions, Ask!

Communication issues and management of it, can branch into almost all aspects of life that we have discussed thus far. We get told about having clear communications. But in a marital status, we sometimes forget that our partner is after all a separate individual. His/her brain is not going to function in a manner similar to yours all the time.

Focusing on the intent and impact is always very useful once you have decided to take the first step and ask.

1. "Was it your intent to hurt my feelings today when you said...? "

2. "Just wanted to let you know that it really bothered me when you said ... Maybe it was the intent but I did not appreciate the words used."

Conveying the message to your spouse about the way you interpreted his/her delivery is also helpful for them. This is especially true as you start the journey. No matter how much you tell yourself that you know each other very well, there is always room to learn more. As the two of you are discovering each other, it might be helpful to convey the short sweet messages and clarifications to understand more and reveal some.

If it makes you feel any better, as far as communication goes, it only gets better. We bruise and scar on the way if we don't use the simple three pronged approach of Ask, Intent and Impact, but we learn nevertheless (if we make it).

If you ask older couples who have traversed long terms of life together, you will realize that they have learned to decode and interpret each other very well. They have lived, bruised, scarred and learnt. They stayed persistent. But they learnt. And somewhere along the way, the communication stream became somewhat flawless. They could judge by their verbal and non-vernal communication, what the intents were.

But again, the journey to get to that point is not easy and requires some clarifications and making sure that the synchronization (that we have always heard about married couples) is worked on. The fine tuning helps.

As we talk to these older couples, remember another thing. These couples most probably used a different form and format of communication than the one that you are using today. Today, communication has been made extremely seamless and easy to use. You want to convey an emotion four thousand miles away, you have the use of texts, messengers, emails, emoticons and video conferencing to fall back on. You have these tools at your fingertips and disposal. Use them to your advantage. Advice will be not to over use them such that you lose the sensuality of touch, feel, insecurities and emotions but use them nonetheless. But stay in touch and that will help you get synched.

Careers and conflict they create in your personal life

Managing career and home life is never an easy task. We have all been told that. And we all make the mistake of thinking that it won't happen to us. After all don't we all consider ourselves to be super humans?

In reality, balancing careers and home life can be very challenging. It's not only true for women (especially later in life when you embrace motherhood), it is also very difficult for men. This is especially true if you are ambitious and want to advance your career rapidly.

As singles, we are responsible only for ourselves. We can dedicate all the time that we need to our careers and reap the benefits of it as we please. But when you start the journey in a duo status, you suddenly become responsible for someone else in your life.

You are responsible to make sure you are spending time at home. You are responsible to ascertain that your career is secure and you are not taking undue risks (after all, there is a future to create). You are responsible for the proper savings and insurance policies. More significantly, you are responsible to take care of a unit (not just yourself). You have to be sensible about the decisions you make.

But imagine going to your boss and saying "now that I have tied the knot, I will need some more flexible hours and considerations for my time constraints while you keep me under consideration for promotions and salary hikes." Yes, that conversation will not end well for you. Your boss might not say anything, but you have basically sealed your fate with this firm.

"Career minded" and "Normal Home life" seems to be oxymoronic in a sentence. But you are asked to make it happen. The fun is all the more heightened when you and your spouse both have ambitious career goals but also want all the things "normal" people do in their home. You might as well have asked to be domiciled on the moon.

Let us imagine the first stage.

You are married to the love of your life (and somewhat to your career). You loved him/her because they were career minded, ambitious and a go-getter. After marriage, life goes on. You both devote yourself to your career just like you were when you were single. After the crazy work days, when you come home, both of you are exhausted but happy to see each other. You turn on the fireplace, get yourselves a glass of wine each and order in. Some days you step out and meet your other riends just like you used to when you were dating or single and happy to mingle. Life couldn't be better because now you have the right person to share those evenings with after you have had the most adrenalin rushing day in office. (Let's not even touch the idea that the two of you might be in the same office)

But there will be days when your work commitments go beyond the design you had in your mind. You get called in for a late last minute meeting or have to rush to another city on a moment's notice. Earlier, you could just pack and go or stay as late as needed. Now, you have to let another person know your whereabouts. You have to make sure that this other person is aware of your exact location, your exact coordinates (more for safety than for keeping tabs) and your exact expected time for return (well, almost exact. You still manage to do so and sometimes even willingly. You love the fact that now somebody cares for you and will be waiting when you return home.

Some take it well, others might struggle. For those who struggle with circling back home to making sure your better half is well-informed or those who sometimes struggle with the questioning that comes if you somehow forget to do so, tell yourself that you willingly signed up for this. This is part of the package. You can't cherry pick what you like or dislike about the marital expectations. But what you can do is manage expectations and set ground rules (but be and ask for flexibility on the rules).

If your job is such that you have to provide hundred and twenty percent flexibility for the job, be upfront and tell your spouse about it. Put their mind to ease. They will appreciate you working hard (after all you are doing so for the family unit now versus selfishly for yourself). Getting your spouse to be on board with the fact that your hours might be odd, your schedule might flip on its head and you might be unavailable for him/her at times when work calls, but letting them know how much you love them, puts their mind at ease. They are now part of this process versus an uninformed by stander. They will recognize your commitment to the future you are creating along with them. It makes it a lot easier when both of you are on that fast track career. Getting your spouse apprised of your career demands, helps them fully comprehend the realm in which you enter on your work field. It also helps them feel less

1. Insecure

2. Unattended

3. Ignored and

4. Disrespected

It is amazing how much cooperation and encouragement you might receive when your spouse fully understands that you are sensitive to their psyche but want to fulfil your future goals.

Hopefully, you will never take undue advantage of the cooperation and encouragement.

Also, hopefully, you are also fully utilizing the avenues of communication that are made available to you. Consider sending a selfie to your love when you are taking a short bathroom break. Consider leaving a voice mail just to say "you love them" when you run for coffee. Consider texting a small message about the night before and how it runs through your mind (when you are not fully engaged in the business conversations around you). Those small touch points with your love during your busy career day helps them feel "in-touch".

Now let's consider the other side when one of you is in charge of the career moves while the other has taken charge of the home front. This is where you need to utilize the communication mechanics even more. This is when you have to manage the expectations and gain flexibility to a whole new level. You are busy at work and churning the career wheel while your love is making the house a home for the two of you.

You receive the texts, the calls and the emails but your frame of mind might be on a different paradigm all together. Your patience is not at its best and you are strained for time. You don't have the time to deal with the "in-touch" aspects when you are running at two hundred miles per hour to ascertain that your boss knows that you are the successor to the throne. So, what do you do when your spouse makes the attempts to stay in touch, to carve out time on your schedule or to have expectations of a normal-couple life?

You snap. You snarl. And you become occasionally nasty. A spark that sometimes dies as a spark but can occasionally take a turn for the worst to become the forest fire. Your thoughts:

1. Doesn't understand what I have to deal with. Staying at home does that to you.

2. Has suddenly switched to being a complete home body. Whatever happened to the career minded person I fell in love with?

3. I can't keep working this hard and stop time-and-again to provide updates on why I am so busy. Why isn't there

understanding and appreciation for what I do? I am not doing this just for myself, am I?

4. These constant messages are distracting. I then feel I should also respond but I really don't have time to be distracted from work right now.

You are well within your rights to feel the way you do. After all, you did sign up for the career and taking the foot off the accelerator will only have negative consequences in the long run. And of course, you also presume that your spouse should be supportive to the effort it takes to keep that career machine moving forward. But now here is some food for thought for the likes of you or the ones who see themselves taking up the described shape.

As an example (and not trying to be sexist here), the husband has to travel and run around the world to show his commitment to his company. He is progressing on his career ladder fast and furious. He is successful and in line for many more promotions. As he travels, his social engagements also increase. Dinner with colleagues, lunches with clients/customers and of course the after hour drinks and golf games where everything important gets decided and discussed. Wife has taken a step back in career to make a home. After two kids, her life now revolves around the home and the kids. But she misses the time the two of them used to spend together. With his overseas travels, communication becomes all the more difficult. The time difference and his crazy schedule makes it difficult to stay connected.

They discover the art of texting. They text and "WhatsApp" each other whenever they can. But soon expectations arise from those mediums as well. "Why didn't he respond to my text from last night?", "He checked WhatsApp, but he didn't write back." It doesn't help that these days these apps also make it impossible to hide the time, date and living moment when you were online or where your eyes were. They might as well scan the retina to reveal to the world your whereabouts. For him, soon, it becomes haunting. He complains that she is always haunting him. He has things to do and things on mind. He doesn't want to circle back all the time even via texts. "If only she worked, she would know the demands of my work." Or "how will she know the value of a double income family? I have to worry about the security of the household." All valid from both points of view. She wanted to stay connected and know that she was on his mind. He wanted to focus on his work (a different adrenalin rush) and didn't want to be distracted. Somewhere he was also losing the patience of having to manage two fronts. And he started feeling that they were losing things to talk about. After all, she didn't appreciate the true challenges of a demanding career front like he did. And when he came back home, tired and exhausted, he wasn't interested in learning about the newly acquired furniture or the home heating system now working. He wanted to rest and regain his energy for the next tiring day. Work occupied his mind even at home. Right or wrong, career growth and office politics came with him back home. It was difficult for her to connect with him even when he was at home and close to her.

In a situation like this, what would you do? I can tell you some of the things that you don't do. Blaming each other and finger pointing is something you need to refrain from. Not because it is not a simple solution and one that probably gives a lot of satisfaction. But one only leads to the use of a lot of bitter words with no useful and productive end result. If anything, finger pointing only enhances the distance that you already feel in your relationship.

Consider the following. For the wife-

1. Make yourself busy. Pick a part time job, a voluntary position or a charitable organization that keeps you

engaged. Mentioning to your spouse on a continuous basis that he is absent from your life will not do the magic. Instead, make yourself busy. He needs to feel the absence too. He needs to know that there is a life for you, outside what the two of you share. It's not a trick or a shenanigan. It is actually a well-tried and tested method that things that are not easily available to us, makes us want it more. Consider making yourself a little bit unavailable.

2. Try not to reach out to him so regularly. Let your thought pop in his mind. A little bit of distance and a little bit of "blank spaces" makes the questions appear. "Where is she?" "Is she ok?" "Why hasn't she called or texted me?" These thoughts are not bad, they are just human. If you are always presenting yourself to him (virtually or otherwise), he is not getting the time to miss you. He will miss you when he is ready to miss you. He has things on his mind and he knows you are around. On the other hand, if you are busy and give him the space he needs to flourish in his passion and career, he will find time to think about you. He will have questions pop into his mind about you. You are now the part of his thought he welcomes, not intrudes. He had to turn his focus towards you. And isn't

that what you were looking for. A little bit of absence helps the hearts.

3. Find your own passion and be true to it. Your decision to stay at home and make it a heaven for the two of you was your decision. You have to be true to yourself and your decision. Instead of turning the focus on him, turn it towards yourself. Where is your adrenalin rush? What gets you all pumped up? Focus your energy on that and channel your mind to this cause. Not only will you be doing yourself justice, you will also find the purpose that he was seeking for you. It helps you answer his questions regarding your understanding of the outside world. But more than answering his question, you will find the purpose that you are true to. Remember again, you didn't come to this earth to be just a home-maker. You have another purpose in life. Find that purpose.

4. For those who wonder (like the wife) about how to manage the kids, remember the life that you give them, is the life they know. You have benchmarks in your mind, from the conditioning that this world has cast on you. Your children need to see their parents be happy. Not remorseful and unhappy in the process of rearing them. Use avenues

available to you in the outside world. Nannies, child care, schools, after care, grand-parents, friends, relatives and other activities that keep your child engaged in a safe and nourishing environment but also allow you to stay busy and in pursuit of your passion, are avenues that you need to explore. Even if your passion is at home, figure out a way to give yourself a "me" time whereby you are able to disengage yourself from the "we" world you are creating and lets you into a world where you focus your energy on yourself.

Many married people will find the above mentioned techniques "selfish" or "self-centered". After all, aren't women meant to first focus on the family? Conditioning speaking again. Women first have to be happy to create the "family". If in the process of making the family, the woman ends up being miserable, nobody in that family is going to be happy. That's purely hypocritical thinking. The wife is important, the mother is important but the "WOMAN" is more important than the others. If she is not happy, she will not make anybody happy.

Now for the husband, what would you do?

1. Consider carving out some time for yourself first. Not for the family or for your company but for yourself. If you get pulled into this rat race where you are so engaged in your work 24/7, you will be a sprint runner but not a marathon winner. And to harp on a cliché (but a very true one), life is a marathon and not a sprint. Save your energy and your focus on the larger goal. In doing so, you will realize that you need the occasional "time out" for yourself. And who else to share those moments with than the love of your life. Head out for a date, a drink, a drive or a raunchy evening out with your girl. If you stop putting her in the category of a "wife" all the time, you will realize this is still the "girl love" that makes your heart skip a beat, your blood pumping and gives you the rush that nobody else can. That rush of blood will re-energize you to put more into your work and your career.

2. Now consider taking small breaks from your travel, meetings, dinner and drinks, to flirt. Here, please read me loud and clear; flirt but do so with the love of your life at home. Flirtation is a very energizing activity. A sexy text, a few erotic words or a quiet time with your love (whether she is in front of you or four thousand miles away) gets the

heart pumping again. You need that for yourself more than your spouse. You loved flirting when you were single. Flirting with your love probably what caused the two of you to "click" in the first place. Consider going back to that place where you are just using words, looks and touches to create a feeling.

3. Lastly, consider the odds of stepping so far into your career world, that you lose touch with your real life? Life is about risks. Understand that...but is it truly worth it? Consider taking your wife away on those trips too. Consider taking weekend trips (extended from your business ones) where she can accompany you? Consider a constraint less life?

Life has a way of sneaking up on us. There will always be something or the other to focus on. A career, a job, a child, a home, a yard or a piece of furniture. Don't let these things take away from what truly matters. But before you go down this path, ask yourself one question? What is the value of this marriage to you? Do you want to give it your hundred percent? Do you value it for the person you are in it with? If so, you will find ways to walk around the constraints that life poses. Just keep an open mind.

Interference from each other

I was always too independent for my own good. Always wanting to do things by myself, always wanting my "me" decisions, always taking charge of my life. I guess it's one of the attributes of being the first born. But what that also entailed did not know what it meant to truly "share" the decision making process.

After marriage, I had some rude awakenings. All of a sudden, I felt the "moral" obligation to consult with my spouse. "Do you want this furniture?" "You ok with the vacation plans for summer?" "Do we invite the Smith family also for the weekend party?" Mind you, I started with these questions first geminating in my mind (because that's how I had seen my parents engaging with each other) and then it rolled out into our life (thanks to my own doing) and soon it had taken roots in the household typology. Very soon, my husband would provide his opinion to the choice of furniture, the vacation plans and the choice of guests for the parties hosted (all examples here for thought triggers). And soon thereafter, my genetic calling screamed out that it was against my grain to get so much interference in my decision making process.

By then, I was already calling my husband interfering and controlling. How did I end up marrying somebody who was such a control freak? I had conveniently forgotten about the fact that it had started somewhere with me (I would love to point the finger at my mother in this case but I am sure she didn't really sit me down to train me about seeking permissions from my future spouse). I had started the process as a method of engaging my spouse into my decision making process (as most of us good girls are taught to do). Soon, the process of engagement turned into interference from them. In reality, I had trained my spouse to interfere (and he fell into this training mode like a fish takes to water - but that's for another day). I just didn't realize I was doing so.

But then again, I wasn't the only culprit here. As banters go, my husband also involved me in some of the family discussions/ decisions on his family side. What to do with his parents retirement planning, what health care provisions to place for his dad, how their will needs to be structured, how to coordinate with the other siblings. I had also felt free with my opinions and thoughts. But that's what families do right? Only aspects where more than two people are involved, tends to be usually messy. Soon, some of my input was not being adhered to, which caused me heart ache. Soon, I felt undervalued and not heard. When airing my views, I got to hear that I need to stop interfering in some of these matters.

In reality, none of this heartache was truly required. Carving out our own spaces and then giving the other person some breathing room in their decision making process is sometimes beneficial on many fronts. Imagine allowing yourself to think that it really isn't worth interfering. The backlash of interference is obvious. Is it truly worth it? Imagine giving space to your spouse to make decisions that in your mind are blatantly wrong or inefficient. Imagine being allowed the space to make decisions without the apprehension of your spouse making a negative comment about it. Maybe the two of you can even have a laugh about the stupid decisions later on but in good humor.

Interference comes when we allow it to happen. If we allow and carve out spaces for each other to make good or bad decisions, what have we got to lose. Sometimes a bad decision can lead to more fun than ten good decisions but with a lot less heart ache. Life is a marathon but we focus too much on the small sprints that we want to win. Some will say that some decisions are best taken in isolation while others you might want to consult.

For one of the topics, we had discussed domain expertise. Understanding your contribution to the marital partnership based on your skills and expectations. Similarly, for this topic, it is very important for you to understand when you need advice but not help where you are the main decision maker and where you will play solo. This marks out territories for the marital partnership about who plays in which fields.

I can just imagine my mother wincing at the suggestion of not playing in each other's fields in a marriage. After all, my parents made all their decisions together with very little complaints (at least explicitly and in public). But what she fails to recognize is that she had her faith in my dad but also knew places where the duo would be more powerful than him standing alone. She would be her subtle force in the background that brought corroboration to his stands. But my dad will also be the first one to tell you that he didn't need that help all the time. He just received it. He would have much rather gone solo in some cases.

In most marital bonds, with all the implicit and explicit love, faith and trust, we also learn about each other's short comings. Alongside, since security of the future for one also implies security for the other, selfishly, we also have a vested interest in making sure that our spouse makes decisions that's good for them and for "us". Hence comes the added interest in wanting to know, wanting to participate and sometimes wanting to take over the decision making process. In some way it's a self-defense mechanism.

Imagine your spouse making a big career decision which you "think" will lead to problems in his prospects with his company and supervisor, But your spouse is of the opinion that he needs to walk down his own decision (for his own reasons). After numerous advisory sessions, you remind your spouse that security of his career is important for the security of the future plans. You just interfered. You might be absolutely right but have you wondered what would it be like if your spouse does end up making a "wrong" decision? So what? Who said he was perfect? And who is to judge the decision other than him? Does your love for him diminish because he wanted to make that stupid decision?

We are always so afraid to be wrong that we don't allow the exploration process of what the definition of that "wrong" looks like? Will it really be so "wrong" to have an extravagant vacation that you could have managed at half the price? Will it really be so "wrong" to follow your heart when you want to make a slight "wrong" turn on your career? I understand that you don't want the love of your life to make a wrong decision that blatantly ruins their lives, but a little exploration with minimal nudging can't be that bad? This is especially true for cases where your spouse has domain expertise.

Freedom and implicit trust is liberating in its own form. We forget that we were individuals before we were together. We are very capable of making individual decisions. We just need to know the spots where we need to let individuals be individuals. Then it won't feel like we are interfering in our spouse's decisions or our spouses interfering in ours.

Bedroom expectations

Yes, I did leave the best for the last (or close to it). Bedroom expectations after marriage are a fun topic to explore. I know most of us have already explored how the bedroom scene is going to be before we actually considered saying "Yes" or "I do". After all who would want to get in there to only find out that the compatibility level is super low. Ok, I acknowledge that for many individuals and for many in different regions, the expectations of "the first time" and "after marriage" are congruent. But for those, who don't want to leave things to "fate" or those who want to be risk averse, you probably already know what to expect in bed.

After all the chemistry there was a part of the big decision. You and your love light the room on fire (hopefully it's a room of some sorts). The two of you have this chemistry that puts the rest of the world outside into oblivion. When the two of you are together, every touch, every look, every kiss and every move lights a fire inside each of you. This kind of magic is not possible with anybody else and you know it.

As the story progresses in your life, you have to make an attempt to keep that fire on. Yes, I originally hail from the country of Kamasutra, but believe it or not, we are not taught the sex moves in schools like they showed in the movies. Frankly, I don't think the idea of the story was to express erotica or exploratory sex moves. The idea was to show that love (or the expression of love) should be extended in different forms. For many of those who have been married for some time, whether you express it or not, there are times when you sit and think about your sex life before the marriage and wonder where the fire went. Yes, that fire somewhat dims over time for many. It doesn't happen because you don't want sex as much as you did. It happens because "Life happens to you". You get busy, you get older, more mature, and you think more from your brain than your heart and loins. As justified as it is for the world to continue, I call it bull-shit!

Remember, we were animals before we started calling ourselves "evolved". Yes, evolution entails that you let your neurons speak more than your hormones (for the greater good of civilization), but nobody said, you let those hormones die a slow and painful death. And most painfully honest couples will tell you that in a few years after marriage, the fire dims a bit and your sex life become somewhat "predictable". And that my dear is just wrong.

Harvesting and enhancing that inner true animal instinct in you is as if not more important than anything else in your marriage. A great bedroom story helps keep that unspoken bond that is more carnal, more real and more raw/intimate than anything spoken or otherwise. A slight touch, a wink, a caress will speak volumes, more than any lists, speeches or long hours of therapy. A few ideas (pick any popular website) on how to enhance your marital sex life will educate you but won't tell you the preface, the details or the socially unacceptable truths. The act of sex is defined explicitly but the preamble before sex and foreplay never does. Let's give it a shot.

1. Taking care of you is bloody important.

So, you are either getting married, just married or have been married and want to read what the hell this book is all about. Right now you are fit and sexy. You feel good about yourself and how you look. Believe it or not, that gets reflected in what you wear and how you carry yourself. And without you trying, you are exuding all the right frequencies for your partner to get the "mating" signals. Try not to lose these frequencies as you advance through your marriage. Make an effort to stay fit, healthy, sexy and alluring. Your sex appeal is very important for the bedroom scene. Your toned body, your sexy curves and your lovely lithe look is important but alongside, showing that you love the way you look also comes from other grooming aspects.

Groom yourself - it is absolutely imperative that you don't give up on grooming yourself. Your hair nails, skin, face, body all needs attention. Give it. Do not miss your hair appointments. This goes for men or women. Try a different look from time to time to explore. Taking care of your nails suggests that when you touch your love, you are doing so with as much respect for the other person's body as you are your own. Making sure that you feel and smell good when you join your partner in bed, expresses that you are making memories that you want to leave her/him with for the next morning. But grooming yourself sends this message that you respect yourself, demand respect and hence will give respect even in the act of love making. It sends a stronger message that you don't want to lose grip over life. This tells your spouse that the challenge of mating is still on. Remember my favorite phrase, we are still animals. We still love a good chase. And you are now just upping the ante to let your partner match up to. Is she / he still up for the game where you look and feel so sexy that they want you but have to still "try" to get you. The "try" part keeps the allure and excitement on.

Take care of your physique - Physical fitness is great for your physical and mental health. After all being healthy will only help you in the long run. But it helps in the shorter term as well, especially where sex is concerned. If I have to take a vote amongst couples who say they gained weight after marriage, I will probably surprise myself too. But I ask why? Unless, you have a valid medical reason for not staying in shape and healthy/fit, you owe it to yourself to a body which makes you feel like a million dollars. Why do you want to give up on yourself just because you have now attained the final love goal of being "hitched"? Staying fit and sexy again contributes to the challenge in the bedroom. Your spouse will love the effort you put into looking your toned and sexy self. You love your body and you are now going to allow yourself to the most basic carnal desires with that body with your love. Imagine what a strong message you are sending. Besides the fact that your sexual moves will be all the more lithe and flexible, you will also feel good about many positions which otherwise you might shy away from. Feeling good about your body, instills a new level of confidence in you, which will scream a silent melody when you are in the throes of sexual exploration with your love. It will keep the memories of the times when you two were still sizing each other up (not just physically but for life) before you got hitched. Those days, the little uncertainty if this fantastic looking person will say yes to you or not, had kept you on your toes. Keep that mating dance on as you advance through the marital journey.

Your wardrobe needs a story - Try and make an effort in staying abreast with style and fashion. There is a reason why this multi-billion dollar industry is in existence. A different look and a different style statement doesn't just put you on the map, it keeps you there. Now, I didn't say any of this was going to be inexpensive but you can always find a way to get around it. There are always the brands, stores and places where you can look like a million dollar without paying the sum. Paying attention to style and clothing tells the world and your spouse that you still have it in you. You are fashionable and people love fashionable people. It's just a fact. It might be shallow and materialistic, but a simple fact of life is that people look at people who look fashionable. Why wouldn't they? They are a beauty and people like to admire beauty. But for your marriage, it also tells your spouse that you are still desirable. As much, if not more, as you were when you were single and the talk of the town. It keeps the game on! Husbands (won't admit to it explicitly) love to have the babe in their arms. They love it when others look at their wives and feel even better knowing that this sexy babe is going home with him for now and forever. Wives love the feel of having a sexy husband in their arms. They love to know that the sexy, handsome strong man is hers to love and keep. He chose her and her alone and that's where she belongs. He takes care of himself for her and him only. It's an exquisite feeling. Now imagine that both of you not only look great together but also have genuine loving smiles for each other. You, my dear, will be not envied but looked up to. The confidence this attitude gives is mind blowing and you will feel it. And this feeling is what you will carry into your bedroom (or wherever it is that you want to explore each other) too. Your sex life will shout of this story.

Do you have "your" perfume?

For those of us who are not allergic to perfumes, I cannot imagine why you wouldn't want to use it. As much as your raw sexuality is expressed in your body smell, try smelling good. Men love women who smell good and women love men more who smell of good perfume/cologne. When you get to the bedroom, your body scent will take over the scene no matter how much you try, so don't worry about it. But just like the investment in your own fashion style, explore your own perfume. Go find out what your personality speaks off and you will find a matching perfume. Not every perfume is for everybody. So explore what your perfume story should be written as. Because that's the story you will express in and outside your bedroom. You will hear couples mention that "this is my wife's perfume" or "this is my husband's perfume/cologne". What they implicitly express is that they have now recognized their spouse's personality. This same personality comes and speaks a story in the bedroom. Let your spouse help you as you buy your perfume for the bedroom (yes, it doesn't need to be the one that you use for the office). You have a different personality in office and a completely different one in your bedroom. (Don't get me wrong. They could very well be one and the same!) Spending some time to find out what your perfume personality is will definitely help you connect with your spouse. The sexy smell is another tool that brings a little oomph to the bedroom. You care to smell good for your love. You care to make the moments special and expensive. Your own body will take over everything else that happens in that room but the first step is like the first page of the book you picked up to read. And you want to read that book everyday with the same excitement that you felt when you started it.

Explore sexual adventure (with a twist)-

An aspect of Kamasutra that gets lost to the common eye is that it not only talks about the different postures that enhance your sexual experience but it also educates us about the art of exploration. The human mind has an exploratory pattern. It likes to try out different things. Along with the different explorations that it does in the outside world, it also wants to explore different techniques, styles, postures, rhythms and moves in the bedroom.

The societal norm teaches us to be exploratory to find our "right" soul mate. At that time we are all pumped up to try different things to find the right mate and partly to find ourselves too. We are defining ourselves. Once we find the "right" mate, we settle down and become domesticated. Then we start becoming our parents (or what we thought we understood of our parents). Slowly in our marriage, we start getting into the habitual mode. The same positions, the same techniques and the same patterns. After all, we are now living with this person and he/she knows us inside out as we think we know ourselves. But soon the habits lead us down the path of boredom (for many). Again, how many different things are you going to try in your lifetime, right?

Wrong! Our minds love surprises. I don't care who you are and how uptight, prudish or by-the-book you are, you are always going to be up for a little surprise, especially when it comes to the sexual adventures of the mind and body. I am not asking you to start reading up Kamasutra to train yourself for surprises that you can play on your love. It's more the subtleties.

Reach out when he or she is least expecting, experiment (to the level both of you are comfortable with) with your sexual story and feel free to express yourself. Sometimes the small sexual gestures can be more intoxicating than a full blown Kamasutra move. Letting a sip of cold white wine seep out of your mouth on the body of your partner, a little creamy lick from each other or an elongated cuddle with nothing but sexual desires being verbalized or otherwise can be more erotic than many things outlined in sex books. And then of course, the surprise new actual sexual moves can be the icing on the cake.

But keeping that mating game ready and on-going is something that you need to keep in mind. Life will always happen, but stealing these moments when you and your love are just lost to the rest of the world and in one of your own, is always going to keep the blood circulating in the marital harmony that you are entering. For those of you who are nascent to this marital stage, you probably think that boredom or prescribed sexual action will never happen to you and your spouse. After all, you can barely keep your hands off of each other and the moves that the two of you explore are always keeping you on your toes. Try one small experiment. Turn to those who have been married for some time and ask how innovative and active their sexual life with their life partner is. If they are being brutally honest, they will shed some light that boredom does set in even with the most passionately involved couples. After all we get into a pattern and a habit. It bears on you to break out of that habitual pattern to keep the hormonal levels pumped and piped for your bedroom scene. No matter how long you have been married, keeping your sexual life spiced up can only help you in the long run.

Another thing to keep at the back of your head is if you are allowing your partner to fully express their sexual desires? I know of so many couples who (believe it or not) are shy of asking their spouses of their true sexual ask. The reason that I have found is that they did try but their spouses wouldn't have it, so they gave up on their desires. Mind you, I am not asking you to try something that you are not comfortable with. But there is no harm in being innovative about the asks and modifying it to find a win-win solutions. If I express more on this topic, I might have to put this book in a different category than the "train me on being married" section. Hence, I will let your fertile minds explore the length and depth of this topic but whatever you do, don't stop exploration. Society puts a taboo on the topic of sex, yet we find the sexually erotic books, movies and sites are always the most inhabited areas. There is a reason for that. In the attempt to create civilization, society has managed to put a lot of well researched and well-founded structure to our thinking but we cannot negate the fact that we are still animals and will always continue to have the carnal animal desires. These desires are more raw and intrinsic than what we get taught elsewhere in our upbringing. We just have to learn to listen to these desires and have a controlled outlet for them.

Ending this topic, will just emphasize one aspect. Your sex story with your spouse is one that is unique to the two of you. Keeping it fresh, aerated and spicy is something you will benefit from in the long run. Don't forget the feeling when you met this special person and knew immediately that your bodies felt so right together. That feeling is one that you should keep harvested forever.

Taking each other for granted

This might be the shortest topic of this book.

Most couples will tell you that they don't take their spouse for granted and I call that bull shit. Taking each other for granted is part and parcel of being married. It happens and happens naturally. You don't realize and you definitely don't intend for it to happen but it does. And you are as guilty of doing so as your spouse is. But instead of taking it as a bad thing, one should think of it as a natural evolution of your marital organism. It's as much a part of the institute of marriage as is sleeping together. Then why deny or shun it. Instead why not just accept, embrace and revolutionize it. For those who don't see the problem, let me tell you a small story.

One friend of mine, during a relatively drunken stupor and in the presence of his beloved wife, revealed that he had thirty five girlfriends before he got married to his special lady. He went on to say that he still remembers the ones who kept him on his toes. There was always a challenge with those ladies and that made them special. While his wife was taking it very well (at least in front of everyone else), he expressed that the girlfriends who always posed the challenge, the ones who always made him work towards getting their attention and keeping it, were the ones whom he remembered the most.

Later the next day, when he was sober (and am sure with some very nice exchanges with his wife), he admitted to the fact that he takes his wife for granted. He realizes that she is always there for him no matter what. She loves him, has made a world for him, has given him two gorgeous kids and takes care of the home while he is busy fulfilling his career goals. But sometimes he does wonder what it would be like if he came back home to a wife whom he couldn't take for granted. One who would still make him work at their relationship like those other girlfriends did. A part of me was ready to tell him that that relationship might not have lasted very long since for every yin you need a yang. Two yins can potentially be lethal together. But I really didn't have the heart to burst his bubble. But it did beg the question, why do we take our spouses for granted and what is the solution to it?

After much soul searching, I have come to the conclusion that no matter how many techniques these well researched books tell you about, you will end up taking each other for granted. And frankly, there is nothing wrong with it as long as you recognize it. What you can do is probably keep the challenge on from time to time.

Some of the topics that we have discussed thus far including taking care of yourself, taking care of your sexual story, taking care of your time and your happiness will probably help alleviate the pain of being taken for granted.

In all this, I have to make a broad assumption that you have made the right decision in your choice of partner for life and that this person (or you) will not deviate from the vows that you have made to each other when you walked down the aisle.

But if you do keep this person in your heart for now and forever, you also have to keep the game on. Keep the challenge on, keep your life spinning and keep the chemistry that you once shared with your spouse. Know that the mating game is not to be taken for granted. As for the rest, as I said, there is frankly no harm in taking each other for granted to a limit.

Knowing that when you need to reach out, your love will always be there, knowing that your pain is theirs too and knowing that no matter what happens in the world, there is one person who will not judge you are a huge peace of mind. The rest is then just garnishing. And that's where you can sprinkle the spice to make life look delicious!

You need a break... Is it forever?

In today's world of "LOL" and "TMI" where we find it easier to relate to three letter acronyms than full blown sentences, do you realize what the word "forever" means? Have you ever thought of your reaction to a book that starts by saying "don't worry, this might take some time to finish since there are two thousand pages to it and another two thousand in the making for you to know how it ends"? Or have you sat back to relax with a TV series that basically shouts "don't know how long it will be before we can define the story line for you". In today's world of short attention span, fast tracked vocalization and speedy conclusions, we are asked to make a decision for life and promise things "forever" when we don't even know what that "forever" will look like. We take these vows of being together "forever" based on a few days, months and maybe a few years of good feeling and dreamy eyed imaginations. No wonder we get disillusioned soon with the brutal realities of life as they dawn on us.

It's easy to say it will not happen but confusion happens, conflicts materialize, relatives become nuisance, stress between careers and family creeps up, time becomes a valued commodity and we are left wondering how life took such a huge turn from the path we had designed for it when we started off. The problem hardly hits home that we really didn't know what we were planning and for how long. We think we are planning forever, when the reality is that forever is far too long.

Now imagine that we don't plan anything for any period of time. We take it slow and easy. For those who have kept their ears open for the nuances of marriage, we have often heard the term the "seven year itch" from time to time in fun and frolic. The timeframe for that can be debated but the truth is that the heart grows and grows apart from time to time. You don't really fall out of love but your heart gets jaded. With everything else happening to us, our focus dilutes from the really important matter of the heart. And for some, we grow up and realize that we are a little different from what we started this journey off as. We evolve and our partner evolves. Many a times that evolutionary path is divergent and we are not able to see the energizing, scintillating feelings that could evolve with these divergent paths. We give up.

The problem in this case is we set out expectations too high in the first place. Imagine where we start this fun journey with the most interesting person standing next to us and instead of or in addition to all the vows that we take, we also make a personal promise to each other, to the tune off-

1. Will stand by you but I will need my space and promise to give you yours when you need it

2. We will take this a day at a time and make it interesting and fun just like we were when we were courting each other

3. When we feel like we are taking steps away from each other, stop to see what we can do differently. I will take charge of my own actions and not yours. I will do my own thinking and not yours

4. When we go through our bad days, we will try to get back to the starting point to see if we still feel the raw emotions that we do today as we start. If so, we will work on the next timeframe.

5. You will always be my love and date before you are my "husband" or "wife". I will always keep in mind that I might lose you if I am not the best at this game. And I don't want to lose you today or tomorrow.

6. We will promise each other that we will enjoy this life together the way we define it for ourselves.

7. When we feel others are coming in between the two of us, run! Run together and run to me. I will run with you.

8. When we feel that we are being pulled apart, I will ask "is it truly worth it?" If I ever feel that it is not worth the effort, I will let you know and maybe we can find a solution together.

9. I love you now! I will grow and you will grow. Hopefully we will have fun growing up together.

And when the "seven" or "five" or "fifteen" year itch starts to show its rotten face, re-kindle these vows one more time. Ask yourself if you still find value in taking these vows. Ask yourself if you still want to play another round of this wonderful game where you are vested in coming out a winner. The fact of the matter is that we allow marriages to grow boring and mundane. We love the essence of why we first wanted to get together in the first place. If we can keep that essence live and running, we won't have to feel like it is time for a break. We make marriage a long process where there has to be a provider, a home maker, a security blanket and an infinity journey. In reality, it is supposed to be fun. Once we work on keeping the spice level high, the story a little interesting and the journey somewhat shortly defined and full of twists and turns, our brain helps keep the story fresh and enticing for us. We then invest in ourselves and in the process we enter. Then it becomes something that is embedded in our brains versus something that we resign to.

And when the feeling of resignation seeps in, take a small step back and have the right conversations. Use the useful lists that you have probably drawn up that take you back to the place where you started. That list was to help you remember all the things you guys loved about each other. Time and again, revisiting that list is not only therapeutic but also very helpful in re-focusing you to the values of the relationship versus all the fluff.

And then it is also important to keep in mind that nothing is forever. Especially in today's world of fast evolution, we need to go easy on ourselves. If you think you need a break, take it. It might not be forever. And here is when I reveal the rest of the story of my own marriage.

While I write these thoughts, observations and frank realizations of my own journey, I revealed to you that I have just stepped out of a marriage myself. But it wasn't a simple divorce. It was a walk away point. My husband and I had fallen into the trap of a society defined marital status where the external pressures had been more powerful and we had not been able to keep the focus on the really valued and important aspects of the relationship. When we decided to work out the divorce settlement, our lawyers were more perplexed than we were. We got married together and we were going to get divorced together. We had fun while separating with the promise of living together and continuing the journey with a small break! Yes, technically we are now single but now we are ready to mingle with each other again.

We wanted to start the process afresh with a little bit more knowledge and training than the last time. We have realized that we allowed other forces to enter our marriage. We needed to expunge the partnership of all the negativity that had seeped in and get back to the root of our togetherness. We are still the best of friends and want to continue this journey together. Only this time we want to do it better. In the last twelve years, we realized that we had grown up and somewhat grown apart. Taking this short break allows us to look at each other the way we had when we first started dating. We evaluate each other with the better knowledge of our journey together already. This is allowing us to aerate the relationship and view ourselves for who we truly are. And if/ when the right time comes around, we will be back together but only a little bit smarter and with a more mature attitude towards this institution.

The journey is always fun. We allow it to get dampened with all the societal pressures. If you have chosen the right person, feel free and let the other person feel fresh and alive. Nobody can define your marriage except the two of you. You will know when to take a small, virtual or solidified break, when/ if to get back together and when/if to step out forever (from this chapter of your life). But taking small steps, having reasonable expectations and not coloring your relationship with the hues of what you see, hear or believe to be the "right" approach will help you and your spouse. And no matter what common sense tells you, unless you are happy, you are not going to make anybody happy around you. So work on your own true happiness and you will find love to share with all around you. But the one person who deserves this happy and loving side of you more than anybody else is your partner for life. It doesn't need to be a legal paper that tells you this reality of life. It is for the two of you to design this journey as it best fits you. And you will know what best fits you!

The Institution of marriage

Sometimes I wonder if marriage is truly for everyone. Sometimes I ponder if it hadn't been for the fantastic tax breaks and the legitimacy of your child's existence, would most people get married? Sometimes I am amazed that people spend multiple decades together and are still going strong. But I never wonder at how beautiful this partnership and teamwork really can be.

If only we can retain the beauty and purity of the first feelings that comes to us when we know that we have met the right person. Unfortunately, the institution of marriage also lies within societal parameters and influence. And external influences often are the impeding factor to this lovely union. If adults can insulate their togetherness from the wrong influences and thoughts around then, they succeed. Those who succumb to the powerful forces that test and try this union, are the ones who end up in heartache and heartburn.

Your marriage is your own little island. Nobody steps on that island unless you allow them too. When you are vested in the relationship enough that you will fight everybody around you to keep the sanctity of your island, you will find that you won't need to fight your partner on anything anymore. But you cannot be hard on yourself if you didn't know what to do to protect this island that exists only in the minds of two people. After all, there wasn't a class offered for you on this in school, college or otherwise. You got the best of education about everything to get your life on the right track but didn't get the guidance on how to stay on track with the right person when you meet them.

Our society invests a lot in training us about how to live. It trains us for a lot of things but instead of training us for this important institution, provides us tools to correct matters when things go wrong. Somewhere there is a missing link, a missing training on how to live that life with the person of your choice. I sincerely wish there was a marriage training class that I could attend before I was walking down the aisle. Some class, a course or a session that does a quick aptitude test of my emotional quotient and that of my partner, and puts together a framework of tools, ideas, techniques and strategies of how to protect that island that we were building for ourselves. We allowed too many people and too many external influences on our island without realizing that we were.

Hopefully, this book will allow you to either think or chart out some for your own island. But this island and the institution of marriage is one that needs work and a lot of protection. It is one that you really shouldn't afford to give up on without a fight. The fight is not

with your partner, it is with your environment to protect the

togetherness, the feelings, the emotions and the dreams that you

have as you say the most beautiful "I Do".

---

www.ingramcontent.com/pod-product-compliance
Lightning Source LLC
Chambersburg PA
CBHW031944090426
42739CB00006B/84